What Went Wrong with American Education

and How to Make It Right

WHAT WENT WRONG
WITH AMERICAN EDUCATION
AND
HOW TO MAKE IT RIGHT

PETER WITONSKI

ARLINGTON HOUSE   *New Rochelle, New York*

Library of Congress Catalog Card Number 72-95365

ISBN 0-87000-201-5

MANUFACTURED IN THE UNITED STATES OF AMERICA

TO
my wife, Deborah

Contents

Contents

Preface

IN HIS ESSAY ON AMERICA, THE NINETEENTH-CENTURY French rationalist Renan, wrote: "The sound instruction of the people is an effect of the high culture of certain classes. The countries which, like the United States, have created a considerable popular instruction without any serious higher instruction, will long have to expiate this fault by their intellectual mediocrity, their vulgarity of manners, their superficial spirit, their lack of general intelligence." What Renan saw in the incipient mass educational system of nineteenth-century America was a vulgarity of manners, a superficial spirit, an intellectual mediocrity, and a lack of general intelligence. Surveying contemporary American education, one could make virtually the same judgment, only with more emphasis, since the American educational enterprise has grown beyond Renan's wildest expectations, and has even come to influence the educational system of Renan's native land.

This book endeavors to examine the contemporary plight of American education, and to make some suggestions as to how we can improve it. To that end I have received help and advice from many sources. In particular I wish to thank the staff of the Institute of Politics at Harvard for providing me with facilities and ample secretarial help. Dean Don K. Price of the John F. Kennedy School of Government and Professor Ernest May, director of the Institute of Politics, were especially helpful, as were Professors Richard Light of the School of Education, Seymour Martin Lipset of the Department of Sociology (who allowed me to read several of his papers on the American

9

academic community in advance of their publication), and John Saloma of the MIT Department of Political Science. I must also thank Mr. William F. Buckley Jr. for permission to publish the results of *Educational Reviewer*'s survey of student opinion, and Mr. M. Blouke Carus, of the Hegler Foundation, who offered me many bibliographical suggestions. Dr. Rhodes Boyson, headmaster of the Highbury Grove School in England, supplied me with a great deal of information on the European educational scene. My editors, Lew Rockwell and Mitch Wright, provided me with great encouragement, as did Neil McCaffrey, publisher of Arlington House. None of the above is in any way responsible for any of the opinions contained in this book; nevertheless, they all provided me with invaluable assistance in forming those opinions.

PETER P. WITONSKI

Institute of Politics
Harvard University
October 1972

What Went Wrong with American Education

and How to Make It Right

1

Introduction

A WARNING TO THE READER

ONE MIGHT BEST BEGIN WITH A FEW POLITE WARNINGS to the reader. This is an opinionated book. One academic's admittedly harsh account of the innumerable evils that have beset American education, particularly higher education (where the author's personal intimacy and expertise are greatest), in recent years. To be even more specific, it is a conservative scholar's analysis of the failure of American education to measure up to the *real* educational needs of our day. It is also a pessimistic book, because there seems to be very little room for optimism over the recent fate of American education.

Initially, as a kind of commercial *jeu d'esprit,* I was tempted to cast prudence to the winds and call the book *Everything You Always Wanted to Know about American Education, But Were Afraid to Ask;* but good sense got the better of me, and I settled for the present title. Besides, the average person isn't really *afraid* to ask questions about American education; he simply no longer knows which questions to ask. His quandary, I hasten to add, is yet another reason for my pessimism.

It is not fashionable to be either pessimistic or conservative these days, let alone to display these tendencies in print. Nevertheless, I make no apologies for either my pessimism or my conservatism. For too long pessimistic conservatives have allowed the optimistic educational nostrums of their progressive brothers to go largely unchallenged, while they devoted their conservatizing energies to such seemingly more interesting problems as the state of the economy and the defense of the Republic. During this time there has been such a lot of tediously insipid twaddle written by the progressives that we were past due for a conservative counterattack.

Of course, while I remain exceedingly pessimistic about the future of American education, I am not completely without hope. A great deal of damage has been done to our schools and colleges over the past twenty-five years or so, but if I believed them to be beyond repair I would probably have remained silent. We may be living in an educational Dark Age, but there remain islands of light, which may yet succeed in saving American education from the blight of its present mediocrity. However, there is urgent need for action, for the blight seems to be spreading rapidly, and has even reached some of the islands of light.

It was the great nineteenth-century liberal Walter Bagehot who warned against the menace of the philanthropists, with their "wild passion for instant action." The modern egalitarian philanthropist—the villain of this volume—is even more dangerous than the nineteenth-century breed against which Bagehot railed. This is particularly true in education, where egalitarian philanthropy has taken the place of teaching and studying. "If [the egalitarian] is allowed to have his way," Angus Maude, an astute British politician, wrote, "he will produce an even more inefficient society than we already have. Worse still, he will destroy our culture, with his pretense that intellect and its cultivation do not matter."[1] In the educational context, Maude continued, the egalitarian philanthropist wants all students to have equal educational opportunities, but in practical

1. Angus Maude, "The Egalitarian Threat," in *Fight for Education* (London, 1969), p. 7.

terms he "instinctively dislikes any process which enables some children to emerge markedly ahead of their fellows." Ultimately, as the reader will discover, such egalitarian sentiments lead to the abolition of fundamental academic standards and to the ultimate destruction of education in the true sense.

As standards fall, more and more unqualified students are diverted from the practical, nonacademic pursuits for which they are most qualified, into academic high schools, and thence into college and even graduate and professional schools. In order to cope with the influx of unqualified students, colleges also continue to lower their standards. Kingsley Amis has stated the problem quite cogently: in education, Amis has written, *more* has meant *worse*. The situation has gotten so bad in the United States that the sociologist Ernest van den Haag has sadly been forced to diagnose it as a bad case of "educational inflation."[2] Over forty percent of college-age youth, van den Haag writes, are presently attending college, even though only twenty-five percent of that age group possess the I.Q. (over 110) necessary to profit from a higher education.

It is hard to see how standards can be preserved in American education, since we hold it as an article of faith that in our democracy everybody is educable through the college level. Eventually, at our present rate of destandardization, college graduates will be below the educational level attained by high school graduates twenty-five years ago. High school graduates may have difficulty with reading and writing. And grammar school may be replaced by some automated version of "Sesame Street." In the long run, Americans may conclude that education is simply not very *relevant*. As van den Haag has written, concerning the future of American higher education:

> [Education will become irrelevant] unless faculties realize that these students are irrelevant to college. Yet faculties

2. Ernest van den Haag, *Political Violence and Civil Disobedience* (New York: Harper & Row, Torchbooks, 1972), p. 99.

are unlikely to do so, since they are in the same boat with the students: far more people teach and do research than are competent to do either. Faculties as well as student bodies expand with available money, and faster by far than available talent. Under these circumstances restless students, led by restless professors, will abound for some time to come. The restlessness can be held in bounds—this side of violence—only by the assertion of the authority to expel disruptive students. Without this assertion students will continue to be restless at least as long as "confrontation" is more "relevant"—i.e., status conferring—than study. For those incapable of benefiting from study this may be permanently so.[3]

Of course, it is always possible that the situation may get so bad that the philanthropists will give up, repent of their sins, and then go on to menace some other sector of society. However, it is more likely that our schools will become Colleges of Unreason, like those described by Samuel Butler in his *Erewhon*, where students study Inconsistency and Evasion in order to develop their unreasoning faculties. In fact we may already have reached that stage at several of our notable schools and colleges. One need only examine the course lists available to students in our contemporary institutions to see how *unreasoning* many of them are. As wrote Francisco Goya, "The sleep of reason brings forth monsters."

II

The monsters have been all too evident in recent years. Under the banner of student radicalism, these latter-day Luddites have come to personify much that is wrong with contemporary education. But the student radicals, for all their destructive nihilism and wanton vandalism, are not the *cause* of our present educational dilemma. They are merely the products of a system of education that has been sick for many years now.

3. *Ibid.*, pp. 99, 100.

This is not to excuse the student radicals for their many monstrous activities; it is simply to suggest that they might have behaved differently under a sterner system of education. If our standards of university admission were a bit higher, most of them would never have gotten into an institution of higher learning in the first place.

We have encouraged many of our students to aspire to more than they are intellectually capable of accomplishing. The end result has been frustration, and the proliferation of cultural mediocrity. It should be obvious to even the most casual observer that our schools and colleges, along with our cultural environment, have deteriorated badly in recent years. Anyone old enough to remember the way things used to be in our educational system cannot help making comparisons that are detrimental to the present state of affairs. This does not mean that I admire the kind of educational philosophy that held sway in the United States during the first fifty years of this century, for I do not admire it. However, I will say that it was demonstrably superior to our contemporary philosophy of education, even though it was nothing more than a prelude to that philosophy. It was at least partially educative in purpose.

Today our schools and colleges have become bastions of trendiness, where ephemera are more highly valued than traditional culture. Intellectual deciduousness is held to be a virtue, because it stands for *change;* cultural permanence is considered at best an absurdity, at worst a vice. Disinterested research and study, along with cultural preservation and advancement, have long since ceased to be valued as the chief vocations of our schools and colleges. Liberalism and tolerance have been superseded by the illiberalism and intolerance of the so-called Youth Cult, with its tedious emphasis on *relevance.* Pseudo-subjects and cultural fads abound, supplanting the old curriculum with effortless authority. Students speak and write a debased form of English, habitually lapsing into a barbarous jargon that is dangerously reminiscent of Big Brother's New-

17

speak. In short, our schools and colleges have become the sort of places that concerned parents should be advised to warn their children against.

How we came to this present state is, in part, what this book is about. While I have freely availed myself of the tools of modern social scientific investigation and historical analysis, my fundamental judgments remain personal. My perspective is that of the insider rather than that of the outsider; and while my chief purpose in writing this book has been to inform those who are outside the academy, my motivation has remained that of the insider who, for professional reasons, is scandalized by developments in contemporary American education. For in recent years our schools and colleges have received more attention for their silliness and sporadic fits of violence than for their contributions to culture. The basic principles of academic freedom and order have been threatened. Our educational establishment has yet to take a firm stand in defense of its own existence. As Sidney Hook warned: "Where academic anarchy prevails for long, it is followed by academic tyranny or despotism."[4]

III

Haec studia adolescentiam agunt, senectutem oblectant, secundas res orant, adversis perfugim ac solatium praebent, delectant domi, non impediunt foris, pernoctant nobiscum, peregrinantur, rusticantur.[5]

CICERO

4. Sidney Hook, *Academic Freedom and Academic Anarchy* (New York: Cowles Book Co., 1970), p. 261.
5. These studies employ youth, give pleasure to old age, make prosperity more prosperous, are a refuge and a solace in sorrow, amuse us when at home, do not hinder us in our duties abroad, make our nights less lonely, and in our travels and sojournings are our constant companions. [My translation]

Between my graduation from high school in 1961 and my graduation from college in 1965, American attitudes toward education changed mightily. By the time I completed my graduate studies in 1969 the American academy itself had changed beyond recognition. After my first year as a university teacher, during which I observed the transformation of my freshman students from neat little adolescents into hairy protesters, my own devotion to the academy began to wane. To a group of incoming freshmen, I was tempted to say, with Dante, "Lasciate ogni speranza, voi ch' entrate" (Abandon all hope, ye who enter here).

Had I so warned my students, I doubt that my injunction would have dimmed their enthusiasm, since a matriculating freshman is, by definition, an enthusiast. I was myself an enthusiast when I began my college studies. Of course, the academy was a much happier place in those days. When I graduated from high school in 1961 I had, in common with my fellow graduates, great expectations about my future education. Had anyone told me to abandon all hope once I entered college, I would not have taken him very seriously. It must be remembered that 1961 was a relatively congenial time to graduate from high school and enter college. High school itself was still congenial. The education was every bit as bad as it is today, but the Andy Hardyesque lifestyle that still pervaded most American high schools in the late fifties and early sixties compensated for their pedagogical backwardness. Students were still expected to be neat, clean, and polite, and there were few serious disciplinary problems as a result.

Most of my fellow high school students had never heard of cannabis resin, let alone smoked it. Chewing gum and smoking in the lavatories were, as I recall, the major forms which student rebellion took. Left-wing politics had not yet become an adolescent fashion. My fellow students, who were poorly educated in civics and American history, remained oblivious to most political developments, and very few of them were inclined to lament this deficiency. Although various social protest movements, especially the struggle for equal rights for Negroes in the South, had received a great deal of attention and publicity in the media, none of this seemed to affect my fellows. There was a vague sense of interest in the Kennedy-Nixon campaign during the fall of my senior year, but it remained vague. The popular music of the day was every bit as banal as the cacophonous noises that pass for popular music today, but it was devoid of revolutionary content and countercultural propaganda. My high school education was, in short, very far from being ideal, but it was not so bad as to shatter the confidence I then had in the American educational system.

Things have changed since 1961. Recently I visited my old high school, and was quite literally shaken by the changes that had taken place since my graduation. I felt like a modern Lemuel Gulliver, returning to the country of the Houyhnhnms, only to discover that it had been taken over by the Yahoos.[6] Many of the students actually fit Swift's incredulous description of Yahoos. In a contemporary context, many of them reminded me of refugees from a hippy commune. A substantial number of those with whom I spoke claimed to be frequent drug users. The lavatories, which were once used for smoking cigarettes, had become the centers of a thriving drug trade. Some students popped pills, others smoked pot, and a few even bragged about taking harder drugs. There was a quality of suburban decadence about my old high school that made me feel relieved about having graduated ten years earlier—before the deluge. Still my old high school is not so extraordinary. It is today very

6. I derive this analogy from Professor Matthew Hodgart's Swiftian account of his year as a visiting professor at Cornell University, *A New Voyage to the Country of the Houyhnhnms* (New York: G.P. Putnam's Sons, 1970). During Hodgart's year at Cornell, the university was the scene of numerous student riots. Hodgart dismissed the do-gooding liberal professors as modern-day Houyhnhnms, and the students as Yahoos.

similar to other high schools I have visited in the East and the Midwest in preparing this volume.[7]

All of this has only served to heighten my pessimism about the future of American education. When I was still a high school student the extracurricular innocence allowed for a certain degree of assuagement and optimism. If I wasn't properly educated, at least I was not victimized by the Youth Cult. But the real problem, at the high school level as well as the college level, remains one of *education*. Had the tender and vulnerable young minds attending my old high school been subjected to a more rigorous education, most of them undoubtedly would have resisted the seduction of the Youth Cult, with its sensationalist values and its degrading emphasis on drugs and long hair. They would have been too busy studying to pass examinations to waste their time on the drug scene.

A perceptive observer, even in 1961, would have noted that the writing was already on the wall. In retrospect I can see *how* my old high school succumbed to its present low ebb. The way had already been paved, even before my graduation. One might go back to the early years of this century, when the teaching profession ceased to personify the traditional values of professional scholarship in favor of those of professional educationism. It took a long time to beat all the scholarship out of the American teaching profession, and replace it with the educationist drivel of the state teacher's college, but by the time I entered high school the scholars had been vanquished and the educationists reigned supreme. Under these circumstances it is easy to accept the judgment of Jules Simon: "Entre le deux alternatives: Ou pas de maître ou un mauvais maître, le choix

7. I have visited only suburban high schools, like the one I graduated from. The urban high school scene is even more bleak. A rather horrifying picture is painted by Harold Saltzman, a teacher at Franklyn K. Lane High School in Brooklyn, in his book, *Race War in High School* (New Rochelle, N.Y.: Arlington House, 1972).

21

pour un homme sensé ne saurait etre douteux: il repondra: 'Pas de maître.' "[8]

But when one is in high school one scarcely realizes what one is missing out on in not getting a proper education. Besides, high school students seldom possess the qualities of *un homme sensé,* and the law offers no escape from the clutches of *un mauvais maître.* For most high school graduates, the realization of how badly they have been educated never comes. For the minority, the more gifted students, the realization comes too late. They realize the mediocrity of their old teachers, textbooks, and courses. They discover how much they have to *unlearn* if they are ever to become educated in the true sense. The task of undoing the damage done to one's education in high school is truly formidable, and few ever succeed in fully accomplishing it.

I began to recognize how skimpy my high school education had been as soon as I entered college. Had it not been for my own interests, I would have been condemned to a near ignorance of the greatest works of English literature. As things were, I barely sniffed the classics, which is probably more than most of my fellow students did. Aside from snippets of Shakespeare and Milton (quickly learned and quickly forgotten), most of our reading was devoted to the works of various obscure and minor American authors, whose chief claim on our attention was their presence in our readers. Most of the required high school anthologies were dominated by the tedious fictions of educationist-authors, which, we were told, would improve our "reading skills." Greek was not taught in my high school, and Latin was an elective that few bothered to elect. In science courses we learned a good many facts, but very little about scientific method. There were no courses in philosophy, logic,

8. Between the alternatives of no teacher and a bad one, the sensible man does not have to hesitate: he replies at once: "No teacher." [My translation]

or proper geography, although most students were forced to take driver education, home economics, and something called shop. The history books were opinionated and often inaccurate, and historical methodology was never mentioned. It was, in short, not much of an education, and I often marvel how I endured it for four long years.

Fifty years ago few American colleges would have even considered admitting a student with my educational deficiencies. My choice of "elective" subjects alone would have sent most admissions officers up the wall.[9] Nevertheless, like most of my fellow high school students, I had no trouble getting into college in 1961. This was, as I have noted, a fortuitous time to enter college. The Youth Cult had not yet taken over, and the student revolution was only in its infancy. The Silent Generation of the fifties still prevailed, and most of our nation's colleges still had a semimonastic quality about them. The term *Joe College* was still used to describe college men, and students were still thought of as nice young people. It was, in other words, still possible to devote most of your time to serious study, unless you opted for the less serious frivolities that were still a part of college life.

I had elected to attend Bard College, a small, progressive institution in New York's Hudson River Valley, which had once boasted one of the finest classical traditions in American education. The Reverend Bernard Iddings Bell, one of our century's greatest conservative educators and theologians, had headed

9. Although President Charles Eliot of Harvard had initiated an Americanized version of the German elective system at his university in the last years of the nineteenth century, college "electives" took some time to catch on. I am indebted to my former colleague, Professor Dietrich Gerhard of Washington University in St. Louis for showing me his two unpublished papers on this subject: "The Educational Reforms in Germany and the United States at the End of the Nineteenth Century: A Comparison" (originally presented at the Annual Meeting of the American Historical Association in 1964), and "The Emergence of the Credit System in American Education as a Problem of Social and Intellectual History."

the school during the twenties, and Albert Jay Nock, the brilliant and eccentric opponent of progressive education, had been on its faculty.[10] In its greatest days it had been a major center for the schooling of Anglican divines, and was called St. Stephen's College; but when Columbia University, of which it was then a part, decided to chuck its classicism and turn it into an experimental college, it was quickly secularized, and became known as Bard. "My old college," Nock was to write, "was reorganized off the face of the earth."

Bard became, in its own way, one of the pioneers of the progressive movement in American education. Just as it was one of the last serious classical colleges in America, it became one of the first serious progressive colleges. The teachings of Bell and Nock were replaced with those of John Dewey. By the time I arrived there the name of Bernard Iddings Bell was all but forgotten. In a very real sense, my early juxtaposition of what one might call the "St. Stephen's tradition" and the "Bard tradition" was what first interested me in American education.[11] While, thanks to the efforts of a few wise mentors at Bard, I managed to acquire a reasonably good classical education, my study of the "St. Stephen's tradition" convinced me that contemporary education was seriously wanting. Old St. Stephen's clearly provided a better education than new Bard.

In a very real sense, if I may paraphrase Nock, I graduated from Bard in the nick of time. During my senior year (1964–65), Bard, along with many other American universities, was beginning to experience the early spasms of student revolt. The Berkeley revolt, which had taken place that year, had inspired imitations on other campuses throughout the country. Drugs were becoming popular, and the Vietnam War was becoming

10. Nock, a Bard alumnus, paints a vivid picture of what the school was like during its classical period in his *Memoirs of a Superfluous Man* (Chicago: Henry Regnery, 1964).
11. Peter P. Witonski, "Albert Jay Nock and the St. Stephen's Tradition," *Bard–St. Stephen's Alumni Journal* (Spring 1966).

a subject for hot disputation. Had I stayed on for another year, my studies would have been seriously impaired by campus unrest.

Sensing that America's colleges and universities were in for a period of turmoil, I decided to do my graduate work in Britain. My interest in the classics had been aroused by my study of old St. Stephen's, and for the next few years, first at St. Andrews University in Scotland, later at Oxford University, I enjoyed an educational tradition that no longer existed in America. While most of my time in Britain was devoted to the study of medieval history, I remained interested in the American educational scene. I followed the violence then taking place on most American university campuses very closely, and with a sense of sadness. Most of my fellow students at Oxford could not comprehend the developments then taking place in America, and they joked about American higher education. Little did any of us suspect that the turmoil that had begun at Berkeley in 1964 would eventually spread even to Oxford.

When I came from Oxford in 1969 to begin a career in college teaching, I found American universities to be vastly different from what they had been in 1965. A genuine revolution had taken place, and my pessimism became more manifest than it had ever been before. This book is the product of that pessimism.

IV

"Donnez-moi l'enseignement pendant un siècle," declared Napoleon I, "et je serai maître de l'etat."[12] One might amend Bonapart's boast by noting how easy it is to destroy the state by placing control over education in the wrong hands. Indeed, it

12. Let me teach for a generation, and I will become ruler of the state. [My translation]

is the general thesis of this work that American education has been controlled by the wrong hands for a very long time, and the results are obvious to behold. Education has lately been forced to serve new masters. Where once its chief purpose was to *educate,* today American schools and colleges serve other purposes, which are deemed more important. The schools are used to develop new social attitudes in children. Busing and other noneducative tools are used to "integrate" our society— often at the expense of educating it. Literally millions of educational dollars are spent on purposes other than education. This situation is equally apparent in the realm of higher education, where millions of dollars are spent on programs that have virtually nothing to do with the education of undergraduates and graduates.

My personal sympathies lie with a style of education that is now dead in America, the old classical education. In a certain sense, as the reader will learn, it never really had a chance to take root in American soil. While I do not expect us ever to return to that classical mode of education again, I do believe it to be possible to revive standards in those serious subjects that still survive. This is not a manifesto against innovation, although I am firmly opposed to many of the noneducative innovations that have lately taken place in our schools and colleges. Unlike my reformist brothers, both shorn and shaggy, I do not believe in instant solutions. I am not even sure that there are solutions to all the problems presently afflicting American education. As a result, I have been forced to place more emphasis on the nature of the various problems than upon my own tentative solutions to those problems. If nothing else, I hope this work will engender some serious discussions, which may lead us out of this educational Dark Age in which we are living. As I noted earlier, I am not completely without hope.

2

The Cracked Bell

A cracked bell, alone surviving the work of time, will never give forth the ring
of bygone harmonies.

CLAUDE LEVI-STRAUSS
Structural Anthropology

IT HAS BECOME INCREASINGLY DIFFICULT IN RECENT YEARS to speak
about American higher education without conjuring up a
frightful vision of student anarchy and violence, faculty and
administrative weakness and irresponsibility, public confu-
sion and frustration, and intellectual stagnation. Of course, it
would be obvious that this is an unfair caricature of a painfully
serious situation: but, as many observers of the American educational scene have discovered, it is not so unfair as to be devoid
of any truth. It is certainly an analysis that has come to be
widely accepted by the American public in recent years, as a
cursory examination of the shrinking state of our university
coffers will quickly demonstrate. People are no longer so willing to support higher education as they once were, and there is
much pessimism about the future of our colleges and universities.

All this is especially depressing because America's colleges
and universities achieved their present greatness largely as a
result of public support. As a people, Americans have always
been more deeply concerned about education than the citizens
of other nations. It is one of our national traits, and may be
traced back to the Puritanical Massachusetts School Act of

1647, which held that literacy was the best available way of fighting "that old deluder Satan," whose chief goal, according to the Puritans, was to keep the children of the Bay Colony from a knowledge of the Scriptures. Only a few years later, in 1636 to be exact, the General Court of the Massachusetts Bay Colony voted "to give 400 pounds towards a schoale or colledge," eventually to be known as Harvard, thanks mainly to the generosity of one John Harvard, "a godly gentleman and a lover of Learning," whom it pleased God "to stir up . . . to give one half of his estate (it being in all about 1,700 pounds) towards the erecting of a Colledge. . . ."[1] And this was but one example of the kind of public support for higher education that existed in the colonial period in America. By 1693 the College of William and Mary was established, to be followed by Yale in 1701, Princeton in 1746, King's (later known as Columbia) in 1754, Pennsylvania in 1755, Brown in 1764, and Rutgers in 1766. This was an eruption of higher learning unprecedented in history, with no equivalent in Europe. England's two universities, Oxford and Cambridge, were, on the eve of the American Revolution, in a period of intellectual decline, and were, in many ways, the inferiors of the new colonial institutions.

Thomas Jefferson well summed up the views of most Americans when he wrote, in a letter to Colonel Thomas Yancey, "If a nation expects to be ignorant and free in a state of civilization, it expects what never was and never will be." Unfortunately, the Jeffersonian conception of higher education, as outlined in his prospectus for the University of Virginia, was strikingly different from the colonial conception of higher education, and herein lies the clue to the origins of our present educational dilemma. That dilemma is not a very easy one to fathom, a fact that has disturbed more than one student of

1. Anonymous, *New England's First Tracts* (1643). The definitive works on early Harvard are those by Samuel Eliot Morison: *The Founding of Harvard College* (Cambridge: Harvard University Press, 1935) and *Harvard College in the Seventeenth Century*, 2 vols. (Cambridge: Harvard University Press, 1936).

American education. The obstacles blocking our way to understanding it are formidable. To begin with, our picture of the American educational system is at best vague and imprecise. More often than not we see it as we are told it ought to be by the educational correspondents in the popular press, or by the radio and television pundits. These individuals—saturated as they are with the kind of educationist jargon that American teachers' colleges and schools of education have been turning out since the days of John Dewey—suffer from a penchant for ideologizing and for historical vulgarization, which, it sometimes seems, is largely responsible for many of the oversimplifications and misunderstandings that distort our picture of the American university.

Nothing happening on our university campuses today can be explained in terms of ideology (liberal or conservative) or educationist formulas. Our present crisis can only be understood historically, by tracing it back to its origins, and endeavoring to discover where we went wrong (if, in fact, we did go wrong) in the first place. The student willing to undertake so laborious a task will quickly discover that the history of American education is littered with many myths—myths which were originally constructed to make some educationist or ideological point, and which have survived long after the point had been made. Conceptually speaking, the biggest myth concerns the origins and intellectual function of our universities. In simple terms, it goes something like this: American universities were born in the ferment of the Enlightenment—or, in other versions of the myth, the Age of Reason, or possibly the Great Awakening (as the great colonial religious reformation was called), or one of those great "movements" liberal historians associate with the dawn of modernity. Thomas Jefferson's writings are often trotted out to prove the point. However, the simple fact is that our universities—and here I speak of American and European universities (including the British plate-glass variety)—owe *nothing,* save a lot of trendy courses, to any of these "modern" epochs. Nor do they owe anything to the spiritual descendants of these periods, the doyens of the Old Left, and the with-it philosophes of the New Left—and that includes Marx, Mao, Malcolm (X, that is), and Marcuse!

Like Harvard and the other colonial institutions, the idea of the American university is a good deal older than some of the current crop of educationists would have us believe. Ideally one ought not to have to make this point; one certainly wouldn't have needed to make it to, say, Cotton Mather or Henry Dunster, or any of the students and teachers in our colonial universities, for they understood what a university was supposed to be all about. The same cannot be said of the people in our contemporary universities—and that includes students, teachers, and administrators—for a very simple reason: our American universities have lost their way, they have taken a bad turn and, as a result, lost sight of their primary educational mission. This did not happen recently; it happened almost at the beginning of our nation, and quickly led even our best universities to abandon the goals for which they historically stood. Instead of being dedicated to what Hastings Rashdall has called "the consecration of Learning,"[2] they have become places of vocational instrumentalism, capriciously devoted to style and ephemeral taste, contemporary to the point of slavishness; and therein, it seems, lies the essence of their present sad plight.

In the context of our present period of campus unrest, with all its accompanying revolutionary rhetoric, it is instructive to recall that universities originated in a period that had no use for such rhetoric. Like so many things we value in our civilization, universities are a product of the Middle Ages—a time that was so different, and yet so similar to our own. It is not surprising that the modern ideologue would prefer to trace the university's origins to some more intellectually kindred period; and it

2. Hastings Rashdall, *The Universities of Europe in the Middle Ages,* 3 vols. (Oxford: Oxford University Press, 1936), 3:442.

saddens him to learn that the ancient Greeks and Romans had no such institutions, that the Academy gave no degrees, that the philosophers of the Enlightenment preferred the comfort of the great salons and coffeehouses to the disciplined classicism of the eighteenth-century universities. But it remains that universities are a product of the Middle Ages, which, in the words of the late Charles Homer Haskins, "created the university tradition of the modern world, that common tradition which belongs to all our institutions of higher learning, the newest as well as the oldest, and which all college and university men should cherish."[3] The medieval university, as Rashdall put it, was the school of the modern spirit.

Of course, the universities of the Middle Ages were quite different from our modern institutions. Seventeenth-century Harvard was far closer to the medieval ideal than modern Berkeley, in that it was, in Pasquier's phrase, "built on men" *(bâtier en hommes)*, without the vast endowments, massive libraries, complex laboratories, and professional athletic plants we have come to associate with university life. What the twelfth and thirteenth centuries did invent was a system of organized education, with formalized courses and colleges, examinations, commencements, and degrees; and it is this that our modern universities have inherited and built upon. But how many of our contemporary educationists now realize their debt to these old institutions? As Albert Jay Nock once noted, while lamenting the sad state of university education in America: "[Our American] educators had not heard of the *Ratio Studiorum* [of Acquaviva] . . . I suspect they were not sure whether Acquaviva was the hero of Rossini's opera or the name of a Pullman car."[4]

Our colonial universities were, like the medieval universi-

3. C. H. Haskins, *The Rise of Universities* (Ithaca: Cornell University Press, 1957), p. 3.
4. A. J. Nock, *The Memoirs of a Superfluous Man* (Chicago: Henry Regnery, 1964), p. 88.

ties, "built on men." The *trivium* (grammar, rhetoric, and logic) and the *quadrivium* (arithmetic, astronomy, geometry, and music), with their emphasis on the mastery of such humane *disciplines* as linguistic and mathematical thinking, were quickly adopted by these institutions. A student entering Harvard in the seventeenth or eighteenth century really knew his Cicero. What's more, he was expected to "make and speake true Latine in Verse and Prose *suo ut aiunt Marte"* (by himself), and to know the various Greek declensions and conjugations.[5] There were no electives, no courses in home economics, business administration, sociology, or baton twirling. Perhaps the only major difference between colonial Harvard and medieval Paris was the staunch Puritan emphasis on Hebrew: students were expected to translate the Old Testament from Hebrew into Greek at morning prayer, and the New Testament from English into Greek at evening prayer. Aside from this added qualification, any student at colonial Harvard could have easily gotten on in medieval Paris. Classes, of course, were taught mainly in Latin, as was the custom in the medieval universities.

It goes without saying that there were those who were unhappy with all this medieval classicism, pragmatic individuals who *believed* passionately in "education" without actually understanding the fundamental differences between education and mere training. Thomas Jefferson, for all his genius, was such an individual, and he was very far from being alone in his opinions. After all, there was much that needed doing as the new nation moved into the nineteenth century, and it was apparent to the pragmatic Jefferson and his followers that the *trivium* and the *quadrivium* simply were not utilitarian enough to be of any use. There were roads, canals, and bridges that needed building, a frontier that had to be tamed, and a

5. Samuel Eliot Morison, *The Builders of the Bay Colony* (Cambridge, Mass.: Riverside Press, 1936), p. 205.

thousand other technical tasks that were begging to be done before the United States could reach its potential greatness; and so, over one hundred years before John Dewey ever got around to expounding the metaphysical virtues of instrumentalism to the leaders of American education, American education had begun to move away from its early classicism toward the instrumental approach, which has prevailed, with few exceptions, until the present day. In the Morrill Act of 1862, which sought to establish one college in every state for instruction in "such branches of learning as are related to agriculture and the mechanic arts . . . [and] to promote liberal and practical education of the industrial classes in the several pursuits and professions of life," the instrumentalism that Jefferson had envisaged in his proposal for the University of Virginia took root and became the norm for higher education in America. Such classicism as managed to survive the new instrumentalism was left to wither away on isolated and ignored campuses.

The resulting transformation of the American university was eloquently described by Albert Jay Nock, himself an unapologetic advocate of the old classicism:

> . . . The old regime's notion that education is in its nature selective, the peculium of a well-sifted elite, was swept away and replaced by the popular notion that everybody should go to school, college, university, and should have every facility afforded for studying anything that anyone might wish to choose. Our institutions grew to enormous size; the country's student population exceeded anything ever known. Gifts, grants, subsidies, endowments, brought in an incredible flow of money; and our system at once began to take on the aspect of a huge bargain counter or a modern drug-store. . . . After its preliminary clean sweep of the old regime, the succeeding period has been one of incessant and unsuccessful tinkering with the mechanics of the new.
>
> [The theory of the new educational revolution] was based on a flagrant popular perversion of the doctrines of equality and democracy. . . . Under this [new] . . . system, as John Stuart Mill said, the test of the great mind is its power of

agreement with the opinions of small minds. . . . An equalitarian and democratic regime [in education] must . . . assume, tacitly or avowedly, that everybody is educable.

The theory of the old regime was directly contrary to this. [It] did not see that doctrines of equality and democracy had any footing in the premises. . . . [It] did not pretend to believe that everybody is educable, for [it] . . . knew on the contrary, that very few are educable, very few indeed.[6]

Nock was not alone in his pessimism. Egalitarian instrumentalism seemed to have triumphed beyond the wildest dreams of Jefferson and Horace Mann. John Dewey had published his *Democracy and Education* in 1916, and the progressive establishment seemed quite ready to follow Dewey down the egalitarian path. But at the very moment when the forces of the new regime seemed to have reached their intellectual apotheosis, leading conservative educators began to join forces with Nock in an attempt to breath new life into the old classical university. Such men as Irving Babbitt, Charles Eliot Norton, Paul Elmer More, Bernard Iddings Bell, and later Russell Kirk, proceeded to erect a formidable defense of the old idea of a university, criticizing, at the same time, new trends in American higher education.[7] To them the twentieth-century university was a hollow shell of what it ought to be, retaining only the name *university,* and such odd traditional accoutrements as academic garb (for ceremonial occasions *only*) and old-fashioned degrees. The critics of Deweyism had all read Frederick Jackson Turner on the closing of the American frontier, which had been the main excuse, they argued, for the rise of instru-

6. Nock, *op. cit.,* pp. 85–116.
7. Of particular interest is John Dewey's polemic against Nock's *Theory of Education in the United States,* which appeared in the *New Republic* (April 13, 1932), pp. 242–44. "Since anything Mr. Nock writes is worth pondering both for its style . . . and substance," Dewey wrote, "it is to be hoped that the extreme exaggeration of his book will not repel educators and *trainers* [italics added] from giving it serious consideration." Dewey went on to argue that the classical education of the Old Regime was itself a form of instrumental training—useful only to such "vocations" as the ministry. "What has happened," he added, "is that the number of callings for which schools prepare has greatly multiplied."

mentalism in the first place. Now that there was no more frontier to be tamed, Americans could return to the traditions of the Old Regime, to the contemplative leisure of their colonial ancestors; they could again, it was hoped, get back to the business of educating (as opposed to merely training). If nothing else, they could at least provide the educable few with an education in the grand tradition, while also taking care of the needs of those with lesser intellectual endowments. Such, at least, was their hope; and if it now seems impractical it is because we have become conditioned to thinking that the classical education is no longer relevant to the needs of our society.

The genius of the Old Regime lay in the fact that it was not concerned with practical and instrumental things. In simple terms, it was concerned mainly with preparing students for *living,* and *not* for making a living. The first universities were not interested in training people, or in creating what Horace Mann called a "Common Culture." They were nothing more or less than what they claimed to be: *universitates magistrorum disciulorumque,* a learned corporation of masters and disciples.[8] Such a "corporate" relationship requires no romanticizing or idealization; it should simply be taken for what it literally is, or ought to be. Within such a framework there is ample room for development and expansion, even with something like the *trivium* and *quadrivium* at its core. Not surprisingly this fact was first fully understood in America by John Harvard's heirs.

The institutions that had thrived in the Old World were forced to confront an entirely new and different set of circumstances when they were transferred to the New World. The academic standards that had been so rigidly maintained in Europe could not possibly be retained in their original purity in America, with its implacable frontier. Indeed, like every-

8. The term *university* was originally applied to any corporation or guild, and there were many such institutions in the Middle Ages. It took some time for the term to be applied exclusively to learned corporations of students and teachers.

thing else in the New World, including the frontier, man's very status, along with his institutions, was obscure and ambiguous, lacking the kind of precise definition that had been the rule for so many centuries in Europe. This was especially true in higher education, where standards were altered, modified, occasionally diluted, and even augmented to suit the new conditions. Besides, European education at the time of the founding of our colonial universities was going through a period of stagnation, which had reduced some of them to glorified country clubs where professors rarely taught and students almost never studied. The situation was far better in America, but certain traditional subjects were often as crudely taught as the collegiate buildings were crudely built; other courses taught at the colonial universities were new, having no European standard to relate to, save, possibly, that of the dissenting academies of England.

While our colonial universities followed the classical *trivium* and *quadrivium,* producing some formidable intellects along the way, the end result of their teaching was often quite different from what one might have expected. "What distinguishes the [colonial] American college," Daniel Boorstin has written, "was not the corpus of its knowledge, but how, when, where, and to whom it was communicated."[9] The rapid proliferation and dispersal of higher education in this country saved us from the emergence of the kind of degree-granting monopolies (such as Oxford and Cambridge) that had slowed the pace of European education during the seventeenth, eighteenth, and nineteenth centuries; but it also paved the way for the distinctively American "general" university, with its egalitarian underpinnings, which is both the strength and the weakness—very much the weakness—of our system of higher education to this very day.

9. Daniel Boorstin, *The Americans: The Colonial Experience* (London: Penguin Books, 1965), p. 211.

Today our universities find themselves caught up in a serious crisis of purpose. More and more they seem to be searching for a new role, a new definition of their destiny, and more and more they are coming to realize that there is no model, no educational utopia for them to pattern themselves after. Despite the vestiges of the classical European tradition that remain in certain universities, most of them have become *sui generis,* with a unique set of standards all their own. But our universities are not alone in their uncertainty. The ancient universities of Europe have joined us in facing the current crisis; they too are plagued with problems, and seem to be searching for a new set of standards that will help them to survive in the "modern world."

Oddly enough, where once the European intelligentsia held our American universities up as examples of the evil shape-of-things-to-come, certain "New" Europeans—the technocrats who look upon the Harvard School of Business Administration the way their ancestors once looked upon the university of Padua—have recently begun to argue that our educational system is far better suited than their own to the needs of the twentieth century. Jean-Jacques Servan-Schreiber, the doyen of the New Europeans, has even gone so far as to suggest that our instrumentally oriented democratic universities pose a "challenge" to Europe that must be met if the Old World is to survive; and, he argues, the best way to meet the American challenge is to emulate it. American higher education, Servan-Schreiber and his friends seem to be saying, is the *future,* and, they think, it *works.* All this has led one pessimistic French intellectual to predict that the world will one day be ruled by the children of Karl Marx and Coca-Cola.

For the time being at least we can expect more of the same. Too many of our educators have a vested interest in preserving the status quo. The Trojan horse of egalitarian instrumentalism has been in the gates of our universities for too long. We have admitted too many unqualified students and teachers into

37

the academic groves. There may still be time to set matters right, but for the moment, things do not appear to be going well for quality education in America—or throughout the rest of the world for that matter.

II

Perhaps the most amusing development of recent years has been the extent to which student opinion has been taken seriously by American academics. This is a new development that, in many ways, only serves to augment the worsening conditions in our universities. Only a few years ago student opinion was taken for what it was. It was neither overpraised for its youthful wisdom, nor underpraised—though one of the many arguments used against Sen. Barry Goldwater in 1964 was that he was the creation of an articulate, vociferous band of students, and students, it was argued (by many of the same people who today champion student opinion), are immature. Well things have changed. Never before have Americans been so deeply concerned about what students think; never before has so much twaddle been written in defense of student opinion.

The reasons for this *sudden* interest in student opinion are numerous. The campus unrest that has afflicted America in recent years is only part of the answer. To begin with, America has become a younger country than it was at the time of the Goldwater campaign. The total number of young people—those aged fourteen to fifteen—jumped 4.7 percent since 1960, to 40 million. They now make up 20 percent of our population. According to the findings of a report prepared by the Census Bureau from data collected in the 1970 census, more Americans have had at least some contact with college or university life than at any other point in our history, and that is saying a lot in a nation that has always placed a very high priority on higher education. The number of college and university students, according to the Census report, jumped from 4.6 million in the 1964–65 academic year to 7.4 million in the 1969–70 academic year. All this has served to create what sociologists are now beginning to call an "education gap," far more significant in its social implications than the much talked about "generation gap."

We are now the most university-oriented society in the history of the world. The Census Bureau report noted that the proportion of adults with college degrees has tripled since 1940. The proportion of those with at least one or more years of college has more than doubled since 1940, going from 13 to 31 percent of the national population. The proportion of those with at least a high school diploma has risen from 38 to 75 percent of the population during this same period. This expansion of the educated population is something that cuts across traditional racial and cultural lines, and permeates every sector of our society. There has, for example, been a great influx of blacks into our colleges and universities since 1964. In the past ten years black college students jumped from 5 to 7 percent of our college population, rising from 234,000 in the 1960–61 academic year to 492,000 in the 1969–70 academic year.[10]

College students now make up such a large segment of our society that they almost *have* to be taken seriously. With the advent of the eighteen-year-old voter even our political parties will be forced to take them more seriously than they have in the past. This does not mean that the public in general is happy with this new set of circumstances. A recent Gallup poll revealed that students as a class are the most unpopular group in America. This, it should be emphasized, is nothing new. Students have never been very popular. Universities, it has often been said, would be far happier places without them. One medieval scholar described the students of his day in words that might easily slip from the modern tongue: "The student's heart

10. Blacks presently compose 11 percent of the population.

is in the mire, fixed on prebends and things temporal and how to satisfy his desires." "They are so litigious and quarrelsome," remarked another medieval clerk, "that there is no peace with them; wherever they go, be it Paris or Orleans, they disturb the country, their associates, even the whole university."[11] From the beginning, in our own country, they have never been as peaceful and popular as one would have them. Such examples of student unrest as the Rotten Cabbage Rebellion at Harvard in 1807, Yale's Firemen's Riots of 1841 and 1854 (during which several students and firemen were actually killed), and the great nineteenth-century struggles between Dartmouth and Norwich Colleges are but examples of early campus unrest in America. King Solomon was correct when he said, "Say not thou, What is the cause that the former days were better than these? For thou dost not inquire wisely concerning this."

Politically, many things have happened over the past ten years. Campus conservatives have become a force to be reckoned with, but have yet to make an impact on the public consciousness equal to that made by the campus leftists. The YAF and the ISI[12] remain the principal outlets for young conservatives, as they were ten years ago. Because of their stolidity, both organizations, especially YAF, have managed to produce the kind of alumni capable of working within, and influencing, the American system. The Nixon Administration has many former YAFers working for it, as do countless congressmen, senators, and governors—of both political parties! ISI, with its bent for intellectualism, has been particularly effective in producing a group of articulate young teachers and university professors, whose influence is already felt within the academy.

The student left, while gaining a great deal of public atten-

11. Haskins, *op. cit.*, p. 62.
12. The Young Americans for Freedom and the Intercollegiate Studies Institute, both conservative student organizations with large followings. ISI chapters have been founded in several British universities: St. Andrews and the London School of Economics, among them.

tion through the mass media, has not been so successful organizationally. Left-wing organizations have been, at best, ephemeral, coming and going with such chaotic frequency that it is almost impossible to remember the initials of the current movement. The same may be said for the leaders of the student left, many of whom were not students, all of whom were so transient that they seemed to leave soon after they arrived. The "instant" leadership of the New Left was, in the long run, more a figment of the media's imagination than anything else. How many people can now remember such "leaders" as Mario Savio, Stokely Carmichael, or H. Rap Brown? Like heavyweight champions, New Left leaders never come back. . . . Thank God.

The New Left has become a force to be reckoned with on our campuses almost in spite of itself: in a less uptight society than our own, its faddish vulgarity, Byzantine intrigues and power struggles, and childish temper-tantrums would have prevented it from achieving any status at all. It has certainly never come close to representing anything even casually approaching a majority of our students, but that is of little importance to them; the salient fact is that the leaders of the New Left have succeeded in convincing an inordinate number of people that they do in fact represent the majority of our students, that they are the wave of the future. In simple terms, they have pulled the wool over our eyes. They have performed a public-relations job of genius, tricking everyone from your friendly neighborhood college president to the well-intentioned former governor William Scranton. Public relations, you see, is what they are all about. In quieter times, Abbie Hoffman, that middle-aged student leader, would undoubtedly have risen to the top of the public-relations profession, which, come to think of it, he has.[13]

13. See John Coyne's *The Kumquat Statement: Anarchy in the Groves of Academe* (New York: Cowles Book Co., 1970) for a classic exposure of the New Left controversialists. "A great number of the flower children are over thirty," Coyne writes. "Jerry Rubin and Abbie Hoffman have reached middle age. But they're still children. Evil children. 'We're going to get your children,' they say . . . And they mean it."

With all this in mind, a review of the development of the campus left over the past decade seems in order. In the early sixties Vietnam was still a "far off and distant country," about which most college students were ignorant and uninterested. The so-called Silent Generation of the 1950s had not yet died. The Beatles had not yet arrived. Eldridge Cleaver was still serving a sentence for rape. Crew cuts were in. Most kids were uninterested in politics. The Stevensonian liberals, along with a few Kennedy heretics, ran our universities, or most of them, with benign neglect. The Old Leftists had largely recanted in the wake of Joe McCarthy, and the causes that moved people in the thirties and forties had long been forgotten, along with Alger Hiss, Whittaker Chambers, and Henry Wallace. Marxism, as far as most students were concerned, was something a guy called Groucho did for a living; and Fidel Castro was a bearded humbug who disgorged a lot of anti-American rubbish.

The left, what there was of it, was reduced to mouthing the cliches of what Sidney Hook has called "ritualistic liberalism." They had no real issue. A casual perusal of I. F. Stone's newsletter, or the old *National Guardian,* from those years will reveal the paucity of the left's arsenal in those quiet and happy days. It was as if old Ike had put them all to sleep. As far as the campus left was concerned in those days, it was even worse off. Liberalism was the closest any of them got to revolution, and the few hardliners, who were mainly the children of the Old Left, were isolated and alone. The ban-the-bomb movement had been imported from Britain in the late fifties, but it never made the kind of headway over here that it had at Oxford, Cambridge, and London School of Economics (LSE). The CNVA (the Committee for Non-Violent Action) staged a few mini-Aldermaston marches, and SANE (the Committee for a Sane Nuclear Policy), which was never really all that left, managed to scare a few students with reports about the amount of strontium 90 in their milk. But strontium 90, as Dr. Linus

Pauling was to discover, is not the stuff that revolutions are made of. Besides, the leaders of the ban-the-bomb movement were not the kind of people to appeal to college kids; most of them were sodden Old Leftists, and *Saturday Review* liberals, who looked for all the world like refugees from a Henry Wallace meeting.

It was the civil rights struggle in the American South that first attracted a large segment of American students to the banners of the left. What Professor C. Vann Woodward has called the Second Reconstruction brought thousands of idealistic students, along with their professors, to the South to protest against racial segregation. The importance of the civil rights movement to the development of a strong New Left in this country cannot be overemphasized. It was the kind of issue that you could sink your teeth into—and thousands did. Some of the students (and their colleagues) were "martyred," others mastered the art of political agitation, still others became activist-celebrities, and a great mass movement was born. Out of the sit-ins, freedom rides, and voter-registration drives of the early sixties emerged a small, well-disciplined group of activists, who were eventually to reject the liberal moderation that had marked the movement in its early days. These were the first New Leftists.

To say that the New Left was a product of the civil rights movement is not to impugn that movement. It goes without saying that the overwhelming majority of those who went to the South to protest racism were sincere, well-intentioned idealists. But these good people—the Yankee schoolmarms and Unitarian preachers—were not destined to go far in the movement. During the midsixties a phrase was coined for them, "white liberal." Their black colleagues were dubbed "Uncle Toms." The growing extremist wing of the civil rights movement, which had long since lost interest in civil liberties, had nothing but disdain for these people. James Baldwin spoke the extremists' language in *Fire Next Time;* and Malcolm X in-

43

spired them when he mused about "the chickens coming home to roost" after President Kennedy's assassination.

The extremists, white and black, congregated around an organization called SNCC (Student Non-Violent Coordinating Committee), which advocated things that had very little to do with the struggle for racial equality. It was, among other things, one of the first organizations in America openly to defend Castroism and side with the North Vietnamese. By 1965 SNCC had become the first powerful leftist organization on our campuses since the thirties. But in a matter of months SNCC did something that was profoundly to influence the future of the American campus left for the rest of the decade. It was one of the many irrational gestures that were to mark that organization in its waning days, and, in a very real sense, it was a rejection of everything the organization was originally set up to personify.

In the name of something called "black power"—a phrase that was to become a household word in the late sixties—SNCC purged itself of whites, thus cutting white radicals off from what was the mainstream of the student protest industry. Since there were at the time considerably more whites than blacks in SNCC, this act of excommunication totally changed the sociology of the campus left. SNCC survived a little longer as a kind of Non-Student Violent Coordinating Committee, advocating anti-Semitism, pan-Africanism, urban guerrilla warfare, and Castroism. As for the white majority, it simply acquiesced to the wishes of the blacks, docilely and without a word of protest. For the time being it had no place to go, and so most went nowhere. A few drifted into the budding antiwar movement, which had yet to make a real splash; some attended the 1966 New Politics Convention at Chicago's Palmer House, where they groveled at the feet of the SNCC leaders; others simply freaked out on drugs, flower power, acid-rock, scientology, love. Indeed, had it not been for the war in Vietnam, there is every reason to believe that the New Left would have died back in

1965–66, the victim of its own absurdity. Everything was there to kill it, from the bombast of the black extremists to the boring vegetation of the freaked-out whites. But, as everyone knows, the New Left did not die. Rather, it went on to wield great influence in the second half of the sixties, to bring more than one important American university to its knees.

It was the widely felt antipathy to the long, drawn-out conflict in Vietnam, publicized and occasionally distorted by the media, and cleverly manipulated by a new breed of professional protester, that made the New Left a force on our campuses. This is not to say that there would have been no New Left had it not been for Vietnam; it is simply to emphasize the importance of the Vietnam issue in saving the New Left from the well-deserved obscurity for which it was heading after the breakup of SNCC.

While the war was being escalated, the New Left went through a whole series of changes. SNCC finally died, under the leadership of H. Rap Brown, and nobody really seemed to notice. It's place was taken in the national consciousness by the even more radical Black Panther Party, which derived its inspiration from Chairman Mao's little red book and from the murderous teachings of its founder, Huey P. Newton. The fanatical Students for a Democratic Society (SDS)—a kind of White Panther Party—had a short-lived moment in the sun, during which time it instigated a series of violent uprisings on major campuses around the country. SDS went through a period of ideological mitosis, leaving only its zealotic offspring, the Weathermen, to carry on its revolutionary program with a series of mad-bombings reminiscent of the goings-on in Joseph Conrad's *The Secret Agent.*

By the late sixties there was no single organization capable of commanding the loyalties of the American student left. What developed in place of a national organization were a series of incommensurably disparate groups, scattered on campuses all over the country, united mainly by some vague and sentimental sense of archaic internationalism. They all read Ho (even his wretched poetry), Che, and Eldridge Cleaver. Some of them even waded through the ponderously inarticulate pedanticism of Professor Herbert Marcuse, a German Marxist from California, whose cry, "Toleration is oppression," reminded more than one reader of Big Brother's "War is Peace." But Marcuse was not the only leftist to indulge in Orwellian Newspeak: the "writings" of such cultural aberrations as Jerry Rubin and Abbie Hoffman, plus those of a host of equally irrational monstrosities writing for the "underground press," were saturated with the language of *1984*. Indeed, "The sleep of reason brings forth monsters."

The election of Richard Nixon to the Presidency in 1968 came as a blow to the forces of the left. And Vice President Spiro Agnew's confrontation with their leaders, whom he rightly dubbed "impudent snobs," came as a further blow. They had not expected the country to swing to the right, and they had not expected to be stood up to in quite so firm a manner as Vice President Agnew had. By 1970 the country was simply sick and tired of their troublemaking, and President Nixon spoke for the majority when he called them a bunch of "punks." Added to all this, President Nixon generally succeeded in gradually defusing the Vietnam issue, thus robbing them of their big issue.

As of this writing it is beginning to look as if the violent side of student radicalism has run its course. The left has become fragmented and overideological; it has largely lost its big issue in Vietnam; and it has succeeded in offending the overwhelming majority of Americans of all political persuasions. Unfortunately, everything seems to point to the fact that they have done their damage, and are satisfied to lie low for a time. Clearly our universities will not easily return to the kind of normality they knew only a few short years ago. Most people seem to think that we have seen the end of campus unrest—or at least the kind of campus unrest that marked the late sixties. Our educators are optimistic, cautiously optimistic. But Americans have learned to be suspicious of optimists.

It should be apparent from what we have already written that the student upheavals of the sixties caught most Americans—including conservative Americans—by surprise. We simply were not prepared for the kind of rampant Know-Nothingism that has reduced several of our major universities to states of near anarchy. Incredulous adults cannot understand why this most privileged generation of students should have chosen to behave in such a despicable manner. Older people who had to work and struggle to get through college are sickened and revolted by the stories of campus violence, and are hard pressed to find anything about the student radicals with which to be sympathetic. Quite often these people lump all students together, thus further distorting the situation.

To be sure, the student radicals have their adult defenders—usually sycophantic academics longing to sow their wild oats again.[14] Such a man is Professor Charles Reich, a disarmingly obtuse Yale law don, whose book *The Greening of America* tries to defend the so-called youth culture, but succeeds only in scaling new heights of silliness. There is nothing wrong with our colleges and universities, argued Professor Reich: the ones with large numbers of student radicals have become "youth ghettos," where beflowered students are working to rid the world of war, poverty, bigotry, and a thousand other social ills, which is an altogether good thing. Now if this apologia strikes the reader as being just a little farfetched, not to mention sanctimonious, it is because that is exactly what it is. As one of Dostoevsky's perceptive characters remarks, "they always have this social excuse for every nasty thing they do."

While the campuses appear to have calmed down some since the halcyon days of student unrest in the late sixties, it is still too early to say that campus unrest has run its course. While

---

14. James Hitchcock, "A Short Course in the Three Types of Radical Professors," *New York Times Magazine,* February 21, 1971, pp. 30 ff.

there are indications that things are getting better, the relative calm may simply be a preface to the next storm. Even if our colleges and universities are allowed to return to their normal business again, some may say, with a good deal of justification, that it is too late, that the damage has already been done, and that our universities will never be the same. Having been cracked, the bell, argue some, will never sound the same again.

The 1970s have had their share of campus unrest. Indeed, much of the unrest that plagued our nation's campuses in the wake of the Cambodian invasion had been preceded by a series of predictions by numerous educators and politicians that the campus unrest of the 1960s was *sui generis,* and would not be repeated in the seventies. Some scholars, notably Kenneth Keniston, maintained that the war in Vietnam had very little to do with the *real* sources of campus unrest. Keniston spoke of the "red-diaper" babies, whose liberal parents, having experienced the Depression and World War II, had set a series of social goals for their children that could only be achieved through violence and revolution.

While campus unrest has continued into the 1970s, and while there is some truth in the red-diaper theory, it is clear that things are presently a little better than they were. Nevertheless, there is no reason to think that they won't get worse again. One cannot proclaim at this moment in American history, as some social scientists proclaimed in the 1950s, "the end of ideology" —especially on our nation's campuses. However, one can predict a period of relative calm for several reasons. To begin with, most students—even most radical students—are tired of demonstrating. The hardliners in many cases have come to recognize that their demonstrating and violence lost them more than it gained, alienating the vast majority of Americans along the way. In the long run this recognition on the part of the hardline student rebels may prove more dangerous than all their violent actions of the past in that it may lead to a more sophisticated and, therefore, successful revolutionary approach.[15] Left-wing students may conclude that they don't need to destroy the system to get their way; they only need to find a Henry Wallace or a George McGovern to lend respectability to their cause. At that point they may shed their red diapers and simply take over the system.

But the main reason for the decline in student unrest is clearly the decline of the Vietnam issue. Upon becoming President, Richard Nixon slackened the pace of the war by pulling American troops out and Vietnamizing the combat chores. He also laid the groundwork for the abolition of the draft and the development of a volunteer army, and, as of this writing, draftees no longer have to go to Vietnam unless they volunteer to do so. Without the Vietnam issue to build upon, the student rebels have sought vainly for a new issue or set of issues, but have yet to find anything as potent as the war in Vietnam.

On top of all this student rebels have received less attention in the press than they did during the late sixties. Without all the free publicity they lost their best means of getting their message over. This is not to say that the press is ignoring the campus militants. The major American newspapers and television stations continue to publicize campus leftists, but with less space than in the past. This is partly due to Vice President Agnew's decision to stand up to the fomenters of campus unrest in a series of tough, no-holds-barred speeches. Although the Vice President was widely criticized in the liberal press, his speeches encouraged other leaders, both within and without our universities, to join him in defending American higher education against the onslaughts of the leftist hooligans. Before

15. Since the leftist-inspired street violence at the Democratic Convention in Chicago in 1968, student leftists have concluded that they need to win the public over to their cause through slick public relations rather than through revolutionary violence. At the Miami Democratic Convention in 1972 the Yippies and the Zippies (the Youth International Party and the *Zeitgeist* International Party) staged elaborate public-relations drives in order to remake their respective images with the community. Instead of confronting the local citizens with profanity, they threw parties, and some members even had their hair cut.

the Vice President's decision to speak out, few political or intellectual leaders of any importance had been willing to stand up and tell off the student radicals and their faculty allies. The Vice President's speeches rallied many Americans to his side, and further isolated the radicals from the mainstream of American life.

IV

One of the main tasks confronting Americans in the coming decade will be the reconstruction of our colleges and universities, along with our entire educational system. If that educational system is to survive—indeed, if the United States is going to survive—there will have to be a renaissance of standards both in conduct and in curriculum. No civilization can abandon its standards in education, or in any other area of legitimate endeavor for that matter, without, in the end, succumbing to some primordial barbarism that will be its undoing. And yet this is exactly what we have allowed to take place in American education. Our educational system cannot survive if we allow our schools and universities to be educational and political institutions at the same time. Aside from raising and reviving the standards of our institutions of learning, noneducational and ideological subjects must be tossed out of the curriculum. Our schools must be deideologized. If this is not done soon, the trend to the left will continue apace, brainwashing our future leaders, who will have difficulty with their reading, writing, and arithmetic, since the three Rs are threatened by the same destandardizing forces that started our students moving to the left in the first place. The primary function of our schools and universities ought to be teaching and scholarship, *not* politics, *not* fun and games.

3

The Revolting Students

E natura degli uomini, quando si partono da uno estremo, nel quale sono stati tenuti violentemente, correre volonterosamente, senza fermarsi nel messo, all' altro estremo.[1]

FRANCESCO GUICCIARDINI

CAMPUS UNREST IS NOTHING NEW TO THE AMERICAN SCENE.[2] Since the American Revolution there have been numerous examples of violent protest on our nation's campuses. "The typical student of the early seventeen nineties," writes Samuel Eliot Morison, "was an atheist in religion, an experimentalist in morals, a rebel to authority."[3] Emerson had been suspended from Harvard in 1818 for leading a food riot, and President Josiah Quincy had been forced to call in the public authorities in order to put down an 1834 rebellion at Harvard. At Princeton, between 1800 and 1830, six major campus disturbances took place, during which students occupied college buildings and defied the administration to take them back again. Yale's so-called Great Rebellion of 1828 resulted in the "rustication from

1. It is the nature of men, when they have been kept at one extreme against their will, to rush readily to the other extreme, without pausing halfway to consider. [My translation]
2. For the best historical analysis of early American campus unrest, see Seymour Martin Lipset's account in S. M. Lipset and Gerald M. Schaflander, *Passion and Politics: Student Activism in America* (Boston, 1971), pp. 124–158.
3. Samuel Eliot Morison, *Three Centuries of Harvard*, p. 185. The situation was equally serious in pre-Revolutionary America. Columbia University recently announced that John Jay, a Columbia alumnus and the first chief justice of the Supreme Court, had been rusticated from King's College shortly before the Revolution for taking part in an antiadministration riot.

the college of some forty students," a hefty number for those days. The situation in early nineteenth-century America was so bad that many leading citizens feared for the survival of the academy. "The insubordination of our youth," wrote a disburbed Thomas Jefferson to George Ticknor of Harvard in 1823, "is now the greatest obstacle to their education."[4]

Writing in the *Edinburgh Review* in 1834, Sir William Hamilton noted that "the history of universities—in truth of all human institutions, lay or clerical, proves by a melancholy experience that seminaries founded for the common weal, in the furtherance of sound knowledge, are, if left to themselves, if left without an external and vigilant, an intelligent and disinterested supervision, regularly deflected from the great end for which they were created, and perverted to the private advantages of those through whom that end, it was confidently hoped, would be best accomplished."[5] Throughout the nineteenth century, American universities were deflected from their educational purposes by numerous manifestations of campus rebellion. We have it on the word of the radical writer Lincoln Steffens that he took part in a violent rebellion against the president of Berkeley during his freshman year in 1885.[6]

Student dissent and rebellion continued into the twentieth century and such prominent student radicals as John Reed and Randolph Bourne received a great deal of attention in the press. Of these early twentieth-century student radicals, the conservative Harvard philosopher George Santayana wrote:

> [The] sophomores . . . have discovered the necessity of socialism. . . . [They] all proclaim their disgust with the present state of things in America, they denounce the Constitution . . . the churches, the Government, the colleges . . . and above all they denounce . . . business.

4. Thomas Jefferson, *Writings* (Washington, D.C., 1890), 11:455.
5. Quoted in James Conant, *My Several Lives: Memoirs of a Social Inventor* (New York: Harper & Row, 1970), p. 177.
6. Lincoln Steffens, *The Autobiography of Lincoln Steffens* (New York, 1936).

I have made a severe effort to discover . . . what these rebels want. I see what they are *against*—they are against everything—but what are they *for?* I have not been able to discover it. This may be due to my lack of understanding, or to their incapacity to express themselves clearly, for their style is something appalling. But perhaps their scandalous failure in expression, when expression is what they yearn for and demand at all costs, may be a symptom of something deeper: of a radical mistake they have made in the direction of their efforts and aspirations. They think they need more freedom, more room, a chance to be more spontaneous: I suspect that they have had too much freedom, too much empty space, too much practice in being spontaneous when there was nothing in them to bubble out.[7]

During the Depression years campus unrest reached a new peak, especially in the Eastern universities and the elite institutions of the Midwest and the Far West. The twenties had been a time for the absorption of new things, and such campus unrest as existed was devoted to fighting against the moral restraints of the Victorian era. During the twenties the radio, the flapper, the airplane, the car, the telephone, and the cinema—not to mention the bootlegger—revolutionized the lifestyle of the average college student. "The boy or girl who comes to . . . college, and who has been attending movies for the past six or eight years," wrote Princeton's Christian Gauss, "has seen far more life than the ordinary undergraduate of 1895 ever dreamed of. . . ."[8] During the twenties, Gauss continued, the world had literally changed from top to bottom, and "where things have changed so rapidly, society is usually in for a long and often painful process of adjustment."

This painful process of adjustment, even more than the Depression itself, explains some of the forms which campus protest took in the thirties. During the twenties, thanks to the proliferation of new inventions and a new moral code, Ameri-

7. George Santayana, "America's Young Radicals," *The Forum,* no. 67 (May 1922), pp. 373–374.
8. Christian Gauss, *Life in College* (New York, 1930), p. 108.

ca's pathetic faith in the idea of progress reached its summit. Had the Depression come without the inventions of the twenties, students might have simply tightened their belts and continued with business-as-usual, as they had during the economic depressions of the nineteenth century.

During the thirties student protest ceased to be sporadic and heterogenous. Thanks to the inventions of the twenties it became possible for students at a given university to know what students at other universities in other parts of the country, and in other parts of the world for that matter, were disgruntled about. The Oxford Pledge against participation in war, which originated at Oxford University in England, was subscribed to by thousands of American students during the thirties. The Russian-dominated American Communist Party exerted a powerful influence over America's radical students through the American Student Union (which claimed a membership of twenty thousand), the American Youth Congress (which claimed the support of over five million young people), the Southern Negro Youth Congress (which claimed five hundred thousand members), and the Young Communist League (which claimed to have twenty-two thousand student and nonstudent members).

The 1940s were a period of relative quiescence on our nation's campuses. With our intervention in World War II many universities converted their facilities to serve the war effort, donating equipment and staff to the government for research and development and related training programs for military personnel. Large numbers of students and faculty members departed the academic groves in order to enlist in the military services, and to perform other functions necessary to our war effort. The postwar period, due to the passage of the GI Bill, brought an influx of serious-minded veterans into our universities. These new students had no time for college pranks or political demonstrations, and our campuses became calmer than they had ever been before.

54

By the 1950s the lack of postwar campus turmoil led some critics to dub that generation of college students the Silent Generation. It was a time of introspection, and students found more solace in J. D. Salinger's *Catcher in the Rye* than in the works of Karl Marx. Nevertheless, the mood among our students was not conservative. In his book *Revolt on the Campus*, M. Stanton Evans described student attitudes in the Age of Eisenhower as being "permissive, antireligious, and relativist in the realm of ethics; statist in the realm of politics; anti-anti-Communist in the *sui generis* crisis which grips our age." The Silent Generation of the fifties, Evans lamented, was, in a word, liberal.

II

The torpid campus disposition of the fifties was followed by a renaissance of student activism in the sixties. While, as we have noted, campus unrest has been a part of American collegiate life since the earliest days of the Republic, it became clear to many students of the subject that the campus political activism of the sixties was indeed something very different from anything that had preceded it. At the height of the student uprising at Berkeley, which ushered in this new and different period of American campus turmoil, Professors Seymour Martin Lipset and Paul Seabury wrote:

> [The] human trust that is the basis of any university [has been shaken]. . . . This delicate though often impersonal confidence between teachers and students, professors and professors, students and students, was severely breached. The sounds left by suspicion and resentment over apparent betrayals of trust will remain for a long time. . . .
> The Berkeley Revolt is not just another California curiosity. This new style of campus political action may affect other campuses, and eventually our national political life. . . . The student leftist movements are growing and probably will continue to grow as they demand totally moral solutions to issues of racial discrimination and foreign

policy. The indifference to legality shown by serious students can threaten the foundations of democratic order if it becomes a model for student political action. . . . The danger now exists that students at other universities will have learned how easily a great university can be brought to its knees if but two or three percent of the student body are willing to engage in actions which may force the police on campus. Universities are probably more vulnerable to civil disobedience tactics than any other institutions in the country precisely because those in authority, whether administration or faculty, are liberal. They are reluctant to see force invoked against their students regardless of what the students do. Now that this secret is out, it may be difficult to restrain students from having their way on many campus issues, much as occurs on Latin American campuses.[9]

In the years since the Berkeley Revolt, the Lipset-Seabury prophecy has sadly been proved to be correct. Radicals on campuses throughout the United States have sought, with a great deal of success, to emulate Berkeley, and the American academy has been plagued with numerous examples of violent protest. A professional student protest industry has emerged at most of our leading universities, with its own publications, folk heroes, philosophers, and strategists. Buildings have been burned, leading politicians have been denied the right to speak to students, course lists have been altered—all in the name of radical student protest. What the Germans call *Lehrfreiheit und Lernfreiheit* (the freedom to teach and the freedom to learn) has been seriously prohibited as a result of this new wave of American campus unrest. The greatest potential threat to the survival of academic freedom today, Sidney Hook has written, comes not from reactionaries or chauvinistic politicians, but from this new student left.[10]

Nevertheless, the perpetrators of campus violence have not

9. S. M. Lipset and P. Seabury, "The Lessons of Berkeley," in *The Berkeley Student Revolt,* ed. S. M. Lipset and Sheldon S. Wolin (Garden City, N. Y.: Doubleday & Co., Anchor Books, 1965), p. 349.
10. Sidney Hook, *Academic Freedom and Academic Anarchy* (New York: Cowles Book Co., 1970), p. 43.

been without their establishment defenders. Aside from the Marcusean zealots whose support for campus rebellion is well known, there have been those familiar voices of "moderation" who condemn the wicked "excesses" of the revolting students while praising their youthful "idealism" in the same breath. "I find this sort of cant to be preposterous and disgusting," writes Irving Kristol. "It seems to me that a professor whose students have spat at him and called him a 'motherf——' (it happened at Columbia) ought to be moved to more serious and more manly reflection on what his students are really like, as against what popular mythology says they are supposed to be."[11] Rejecting the view of those who find New Left "idealism" to be praiseworthy, Kristol declares: "My own view is that a significant minority of today's student body obviously consists of a mob who have no real interest in higher education or in the life of the mind, and whose passions are inflamed by a debased popular culture that prevails unchallenged on the campus."

III

Since, as Lipset and Seabury have noted, institutions of higher learning depend upon a fiduciary relationship between students, faculty, and administration, they are uniquely vulnerable to the destructive designs of dedicated agitators—a fact that greatly diminishes the revolutionary quality of their "accomplishments." Invariably most recent manifestations of campus unrest have started over some trivial or nonexistent issue. At Berkeley, for example, the student revolt began in order to gain "freedom of speech," and ended as a struggle to sanctify filthy speech. At Columbia, students revolted against

11. Irving Kristol, *On the Democratic Idea in America* (New York: Harper & Row, 1972), p. 115. The rebel students, Kristol adds, are "for the most part rebels without a cause—and without hope of accomplishing anything except mischief and ruin."

the university's Institute of Defense Analysis and the construction of a student gymnasium on the grounds of a crime-ridden public park that nobody used for fear of being mugged. The leader of the Columbia revolt, Mark Rudd, emphasized, after the revolt had taken place, that the damage had been instigated in the name of nonissues. "Let me tell you," declared Rudd, "we manufactured the issues. The Institute for Defense Analysis is nothing at Columbia. Just three professors. And the gym issue is bull. It doesn't mean anything to anybody. I had never been to the gym site before the demonstration began. I didn't even know how to get there."[12] Nevertheless, trivial nonissues such as these have succeeded in doing more harm to American higher education than all the demonstrations that took place in American higher education prior to the sixties. This is what makes the demonstrations of the sixties something new and different.

Disputes based on nonissues proliferated in the later sixties. Sometimes they concerned the right of the army and navy to recruit future officers on campus; other times they concerned ROTC; the presence of representatives from certain corporations, such as DOW Chemicals, on campus; the right to use campus buildings for political meetings. Only after a certain period of time did the campus rebels endeavor to legitimize their destructive violence by footnoting it with the writings of Marx, Marcuse, and Chomsky; but to date these rather clumsy attempts at intellectualizing their hooliganism have failed to impress anyone, save the apologists for student rebellion.

Despite numerous attempts to construct some form of ideological apologia for student rebellion, the contemporary wave of student revolts has been marked by a singular lack of ideological originality. Unlike the student rebels of the thirties, who attempted to digest the writings of various Marxist ideologues, the contemporary student rebels merely cite the titles of books

12. Quoted in Lipset and Schaflander, *op. cit.*, p. xix.

which they have never read, by authors such as Marcuse. Not only do the contemporary student rebels lack a coherent ideology; they do not even possess the kind of central party discipline that marked the rebels of the thirties. They are truly rebels without a cause, unless one accepts their nihilistic urge to destroy their own universities as a valid cause.

IV

The student rebellion's potential for destroying our universities no longer seems to be a very important issue. There is ample evidence to show that the universities have done much to destroy themselves; they have long since ceased to be repositories of the essential values and ideals of our civilization. The real danger is that the rebellion may continue to subvert the ideals and values of individual students. Whereas the student rebellions of earlier periods in our history were concerned with intramural issues, the contemporary rebellion strikes at the very foundations of our civilization and country.

To date university authorities have not been able to control their revolting students. Indeed, rather than controlling their student militants, universities have tended to give in to them. As a result, many of the more obnoxious aspects of the student rebellion have infected less militant members of the student community, a fact that will become more apparent in the next chapter.

4

What Do Our Students Think?

A specter is haunting America—the specter of students. For the first time in the history of the United States, university students have become a source of interest for all the nation; a source of concern for much of the nation; and a source of fear for some of the nation.

CLARK KERR

ARE THE RADICALS OF THE NEW STUDENT LEFT A SMALL minority, or do they in fact represent the majority of American students? Have our students been influenced in one way or another by the trend to the left on America's campuses? What do our students think about the pressing problems of the day? These are all questions that haunt parents and concerned citizens in this era of student unrest and growing youth consciousness. Parents want to know what will happen to their sons and daughters if they send them to a particular university; establishment politicians of both major parties want to know if they will continue to make converts to their causes on radicalized campuses; concerned citizens wonder what all the trouble on our campuses means for the future of America.

This chapter will endeavor to answer some of these questions, and to present a profile of the students in our contemporary universities.

II

During the 1961–62 and the 1962–63 academic years, the *Educational Reviewer,* in conjunction with the editorial staff of the *National Review,* conducted an extensive survey of student opinion at twelve representative colleges and universities in the hope of providing the general public with a clearer and more comprehensive picture of the trends, styles, and ideas then dominating our nation's campuses.[1] The survey had been inspired by a similar study that appeared in the *Harvard Crimson* in 1959, devoted to the political and religious attitudes of the undergraduate student bodies at Harvard and at Radcliffe College. The *Crimson* questionnaire was prepared under the supervision of the distinguished Harvard sociologist David Riesman. The *Educational Reviewer* used the *Crimson*-Riesman questionnaire as the basis of its own more elaborate survey.

The findings of the *ER* survey caused little stir at the time of their publication. Those were the days when the Silent Generation held sway on our campuses, and when most Americans, as a result, didn't take student opinion very seriously. Some critics even went so far as to suggest that *ER*'s labors were a "venture in triviality." "What can adults ever hope to learn from a bunch of college kids?" one writer caustically observed. Students not only were considered to be dull and uninteresting, but were also, despite their political liberalism, far too culturally conservative, too like their middle-class parents for their liberal mentors to bear. As for the politically conservative minority, it was none too popular. One recalls the way the liberal press, for example, treated Barry Goldwater's youthful supporters in 1964. They were held up as one of the prime reasons for voting against the Arizona senator.

1. *A Survey of the Political and Religious Attitudes of American College Students,* sponsored by the Educational Reviewer, Inc. (New York, 1963).

Well, things have changed since 1964. Student support for a politician is considered a big plus today; student opinion on almost any subject is treated with the greatest possible reverence; and critics of the new prostudent mania are castigated on all fronts. The symbols of youth—particularly dissident youth —have been adopted, or at least partially adopted, by adult society. Deviant hair styles, mod clothing, semiliterate "underground" newspapers, and protest music have become big business, patronized by all sectors of our society. The kids are, to use a current phrase, "where it's at." But for all the emulation of youthful styles and customs by many adults, most people remain confused about what the amorphous younger generation really stands for. Some have even suggested that it is impossible for adults to understand their own children, regardless of how religiously they ape their styles, because of that vague and ancient phenomenon that we call the generation gap.

With all this in mind, the *Educational Reviewer* decided to repeat its survey of student opinion in 1970. So much had changed since the first *ER* survey: the Silent Generation of the fifties and early sixties gave way to the so-called Now Generation of the late sixties and early seventies; a New Left rose from the ashes of Lyndon Johnson's Great Society, radicalizing the kind of students who would have normally remained aloof from politics; the self-confident liberalism that had held sway over the American academy since the days of the New Deal began to falter in the wake of Vietnam; black students became a force to be reckoned with; and the old morality succumbed to the "Let-it-all-hang-out" ethic.[2]

It was a good time to reexamine the opinions of our nation's students, to find out what they were thinking, how they had changed since the early sixties, and how they viewed modern-day America. I should like to thank Mr. William F. Buckley Jr.

2. Peter P. Witonski, "A Memo to the Ripon Society on the Death of American Liberalism," *The Alternative,* vol. 5, no. 7 (April 1972), pp. 5, 6.

of the *Educational Reviewer* and the *National Review,* who commissioned me in 1970 to evaluate the data collected by the *ER* survey, for allowing me to publish our findings here.[3]

III

The institutions participating in the *ER* survey were selected because of their representative character. They typify the heterogeneous nature of the educational enterprise in America. There are big universities and small colleges; male and female institutions; nonsectarian and church-affiliated schools; private and state-controlled universities.

The following short profiles will, it is hoped, give the reader some idea of the differences and similarities apparent in our participating institutions:

1. Sarah Lawrence College   A very small nonsectarian women's college (since our survey it has begun to accept male students) with a reputation for high academic standards, unconventional curriculums, and educational and political progressivism. Located in Bronxville, a New York City suburb in lower Westchester County, the school has a residential environment, and places great emphasis on the humanities. It has an upper-class enrollment of 443, out of which we polled 77.[4]

2. Williams College   A small, private, nonsectarian men's college, with a reputation for high academic standards. Its faculty is very liberal, and its students have a long tradition of moderate liberalism. Located in Williamstown, Massachusetts, the college has a small-town New England environment. We took a sample of 160 out of an upper class of 940.

3. Much of the following material appears here in print for the first time.
4. Our samples are all upper class. The freshman year is an orientation year, during which the university begins to influence the student, and this is not the best year to evaluate student opinion. Our samples are equivalent to simple random samples of all sophomores, juniors, and seniors in each selected school.

3. **Yale University**   A large, private, nonsectarian university, with typical Ivy League academic standards. Since the first *ER* survey, it has gone coeducational and experienced a good deal of campus turmoil. Like most large American universities, it is a world unto itself, with its own police force, shopping facilities, and other community essentials. It is located in the small city of New Haven, which has recently experienced a great deal of urban renewal. We sampled 167 out of an upper class of 3,328.

4. **Marquette University**   A large, urban, Catholic university, run by the Society of Jesus. It is coeducational, with fair to average academic standards. Located in Milwaukee, its students are largely ethnic Americans, and many of them commute to school every day and live with their parents. We sampled 234 students out of an upper class of 4,633.

5. **Boston University**   A very large, private, nonsectarian institution, located along the Charles River in Boston in one of the most educationally saturated areas in the United States. Its vast student body is coeducational, and its standards are average. There are a good number of commuting students at BU, along with a large group of residential students. We took a sampling of 233 students out of an upper class of 8,870.

6. **Indiana University**   A giant, Midwestern, state-supported university, which totally dominates the city of Bloomington. Like most state universities in the Midwest, it is coeducational, with academic standards ranging from poor to excellent, depending upon the department. We took a sampling of 240 students out of an upper class of 14,835.

7. **University of South Carolina**   A large, Southern, state-supported university, located in the medium-sized city of Columbia, the state capital. Since the first *ER* survey, South Carolina has integrated its coeducational student body, like other Southern universities. It is an old institution, with fair academic standards. We took a sample of 274 out of an upper class of 5,810.

64

8. Howard University   A privately controlled, nonsectarian, coeducational, predominantly black university, located in Washington, D. C., and heavily funded by the federal government. During a period of black militancy, Howard has remained relatively calm, despite its numerous radical students and faculty members. Its admissions standards are low, and its academic standards are fair to low. We sampled 117 students out of an upper class of 3,390.

9. Reed College   A small, private, nonsectarian, coeducational institution, with a long history of academic experimentation and political progressivism. Located in Portland, Oregon, the school has a comfortable residential atmosphere. Its academic standards are high, and its students are bright. We took a sampling of 157 students out of an upper class of 771.

10. Davidson College   A small, private, Presbyterian-affiliated men's college in Davidson, North Carolina, about twenty miles north of Charlotte. Davidson is a relatively conservative institution, with above-average academic standards. We took a sample of 199 out of an upper class of 740.

11. Brandeis University   A medium-sized, private, nonsectarian, coeducational institution, founded under Jewish auspices in 1948. Located in Waltham, Massachusetts, a suburb of Boston, the school has high academic standards, and a reputation for moderate liberalism. We took a sample of 181 students out of an upper class of 1,586.

12. Stanford University   A large, nonsectarian, coeducational, privately supported California university, with high academic standards. Stanford is often held up as the prototype of the rich Western upper-middle-class university. We took a sampling of 203 students out of an upper class of 4,719.

Lord Keynes was undoubtedly correct: in the long run we *are* all dead. Which doesn't mean that we are to stop thinking about the long run, as some of our fashionable thinkers would have us do; for the short run will not be with us forever, and things may go from bad to worse. Clearly, this is not a time for optimism about the future of American higher education, the youth cultists to the contrary notwithstanding. In the long run, as all available data seem to suggest, we appear to be heading towards a genuine disaster in our system of higher education.

At the time of the first *ER* survey, things were not quite so bad. Indeed, the casual visitor to one of our selected campuses might well have been encouraged by the seriousness of the students and the seeming affluence of the institution. But there were already indications that the liberalism that had prevailed on most campuses in the early sixties—spurred on by the rhetoric of the New Frontier and the civil rights movement—would become more pronounced and more radical by the end of the decade. John F. Kennedy was in the White House, and, in a very real sense, the old American liberalism was in its heyday. Few Americans would have been deeply depressed at the prospect of a continuing liberal hegemony on our campuses. The old liberalism was something that most Americans, including most conservative Americans, understood; they were not baffled or confused by it; it was simply part of the American ideological system in which they had grown up. Some conservatives even seem to have enjoyed having a liberal majority on our campuses to do battle with, and were more or less willing to preserve the status quo.

Nevertheless, a careful reading of the first *ER* survey reveals a subtle, almost inexorable trend to the left that has become more disturbingly apparent in our most recent findings. In the first *ER* survey, when students were asked to pigeonhole themselves ideologically, the following results were obtained.

Which of the following four designations most nearly describes
your political temperament?

1) Conservative   2) Radical   3) Moderate liberal   4) Politically
indifferent

	SL %	Wms %	Yale %	Marq %	BU %	Ind %	SC %	Hwd %	Reed %	Dav %	Bran %	Stan %
1)	18	36	37	31	24	38	39	8	11	44	7	37
2)	13	5	3	1	6	2	3	8	20		17	5
3)	54	53	47	49	57	48	45	61	57	34	66	45
4)	9	3	9	16	8	8	8	17	5	18	5	8

The reader will note that a substantial number of students
were more than happy to accept the appellation conservative,
particularly at Yale, Stanford, Williams, Indiana, Davidson,
and South Carolina. At the same time, very few of those questioned were willing to call themselves radicals, the exceptions
being Reed, where 20 percent called themselves radical, and
Sarah Lawrence and Brandeis, each of which had more than
10 percent willing to embrace radicalism. The results at these
three schools more or less conformed to what the survey expected to find. Liberalism was still very big on our campuses in
those days, and, with the exception of Davidson, nearly half of
all those polled were willing to accept the liberal designation.

Our current survey noted a major series of shifts in ideological preference. Conservatism had dropped sharply on all campuses, except South Carolina and Marquette, where it dropped
in popularity nonetheless. At Yale, where 37 percent of the
students had called themselves conservatives at the time of the
first *ER* survey, the figure dropped to 13 percent. Radicalism, on
the other hand, jumped in popularity, from 8 percent to 29
percent at Howard, from 5 percent to 14 percent at Williams,
and from 3 percent to 18 percent at Yale.

Which of the following four designations most nearly describes
your own political temperament?

1) Conservative
2) Liberal
3) Radical
4) Politically indifferent

	SL	Wms	Yale	Marq	BU	Ind	SC	Hwd	Reed	Dav	Bran	Stan
	%	%	%	%	%	%	%	%	%	%	%	%
1)	7	9	13	25	9	26	34	7	4	22	7	17
2)	58	68	56	61	66	56	58	54	43	64	61	61
3)	24	14	18	7	18	9	4	29	35	8	25	17
4)	3	4	10	7	4	6	3	7	11	4	6	4

What is the cause of this change in political orientation? Our findings suggest that, by and large, it is a change brought about by the ideological dynamics of the contemporary university more than anything else. In endeavoring to learn how students' political views were altered by university life, we received the following results:

Since you entered college, in which of the following ways have your political views changed? (Please check only one response.)

1) From conservative to more conservative
2) From conservative to less conservative or liberal
3) From conservative to radical
4) From liberal to less liberal or conservative
5) From liberal to more liberal or radical
6) From radical to conservative
7) From radical to less radical or liberal
8) From radical to more radical
9) From politically indifferent to conservative
10) From politically indifferent to liberal
11) From politically indifferent to radical
12) My political views haven't changed since I entered college.

	SL	Wms	Yale	Marq	BU	Ind	SC	Hwd	Reed	Dav	Bran	Stan
	%	%	%	%	%	%	%	%	%	%	%	%
1)		1	2	3	1	2	5		1	3	1	2
2)	9	28	22	35	21	42	47	14	8	46	13	35
3)	1	6	4	1	3	2	2	3	3	1		3
4)	8	4	7	6	2	4	2	1	4	5	6	2
5)	51	33	38	21	39	22	14	48	38	23	48	30
6)								1			1	
7)	1	1	2		1			2	7		2	
8)	4	1			2	1		3	4	1	2	1
9)			1	5		5	4	1				2
10)	4	11	10	12	19	10	12	9	8	11	11	11
11)	4	3	3	1	3		1	6	1	1	2	3
12)	14	9	11	15	8	11	12	9	22	9	14	9

Attempting to break the elements in the change in student

political orientation down to its specific causes, we asked the following question:

> If your political views have changed, which of the following factors have significantly influenced you? (Please check no more than two or three responses.) (If your political views haven't changed, please skip to next question.)
>
> 1) Lectures and/or assigned reading in courses
> 2) Influence of friends
> 3) Personal contact with faculty members
> 4) Increased independent reading
> 5) Independence from parental ideas
> 6) Increased thinking about political questions
> 7) Other

	SL	Wms	Yale	Marq	BU	Ind	SC	Hwd	Reed	Dav	Bran	Stan
	%	%	%	%	%	%	%	%	%	%	%	%
1)	25	45	27	35	41	32	30	35	20	32	24	26
2)	49	49	52	45	41	39	36	14	35	47	52	52
3)	27	7	5	6	5	6	10	5	13	6	7	4
4)	30	26	25	31	38	32	36	49	36	32	24	27
5)	22	20	18	19	13	27	17	10	15	30	16	27
6)	70	75	76	68	70	70	70	71	71	69	82	72
7)	16	7	11	7	9	8	12	15	16	4	14	11

Our findings here run counter to those of certain social scientists who attribute the rise in student radicalism to radical or left-liberal family backgrounds. The parents of the majority of all university students in America tend to be middle and upper-middle class, and to accept *the system* in much the same way as the students polled in the first *ER* survey did. The influence of professors, friends, and to a certain extent a rebellion against the views of their parents, seems to have been far more influential than anything else in altering the political opinions of our participating students. The university's potential for leading students "astray" has long been noted by conservative writers. As early as 1951, William F. Buckley Jr. propounded this thesis, much to the displeasure of his old mentors at Yale, in his book *God and Man at Yale*. In the contemporary context, it is clear that the university experience liberalizes (in the ideological as opposed to the educational sense of that word) and radicalizes students.

The move to the left is apparent in the area of political-party identification. In the first *ER* survey, the Republican Party made a respectable, if inglorious, showing among students, particularly at Yale, Indiana, and Stanford.

With what political party are you affiliated, either in spirit or actual membership?

1) Republican   2) Democratic   3) Other   4) None

	SL	Wms	Yale	Marq	BU	Ind	SC	Hwd	Reed	Dav	Bran	Stan
	%	%	%	%	%	%	%	%	%	%	%	%
1)	18	37	44	29	33	51	33	10	2	36	4	47
2)	50	29	26	35	36	27	35	52	54	26	69	27
3)	9		2	2	3	1	4	2	5	2	2	3
4)	22	31	26	31	24	19	26	31	37	34	22	21

In our current survey, however, there is a major decline in Republican support, with the Democrats remaining strong, although dropping slightly from the position they held in the old survey.

With which political party are you affiliated, either in spirit or actual membership?

1) Democratic
2) Republican
3) Other ·
4) None

	SL	Wms	Yale	Marq	BU	Ind	SC	Hwd	Reed	Dav	Bran	Stan
	%	%	%	%	%	%	%	%	%	%	%	%
1)	41	21	29	36	35	32	22	45	31	31	44	30
2)	3	22	13	15	8	30	33	2	6	18	4	16
3)	4	1	5	4	7	3	4	3	6	1	3	6
4)	51	54	52	45	48	34	41	49	57	50	48	48

Our findings reveal a growing lack of satisfaction with the present two-party system as it exists in America today. At the time of the first *ER* survey, most students polled seemed to be content with our two major parties. Our current findings show a marked rise in those students who are unhappy with each of the two parties. Related to this we noted a rather strong feeling

70

among students at Sarah Lawrence, Yale, Boston University, Reed, and Brandeis that the country needs a new party of the left (as opposed to a new party of the right, which found few potential adherents). This phenomenon is a clear reflection of the trend that began with Eugene McCarthy's "crusade" in 1968.

Which one of the following four attitudes toward political parties most nearly corresponds to your own?

1) The present two-party system is satisfactory on the whole and should be essentially retained
2) The present party structure should be altered so that much sharper lines could be drawn between the two political parties, one being definitely and unambiguously the more "right"-leaning, and the other being definitely and unambiguously the more "left"-leaning
3) I would support the founding of a third party that would represent "the right" more than either the Republicans or the Democrats do at present
4) I would support the founding of a third party that would represent "the left" more than either the Republicans or the Democrats do at present

	SL %	Wms %	Yale %	Marq %	BU %	Ind %	SC %	Hwd %	Reed %	Dav %	Bran %	Stan %
1)	14	38	29	53	19	51	55	23	17	50	25	37
2)	22	16	17	18	23	11	22	21	18	17	15	14
3)			2	7	3	3	5	7	1	2	2	1
4)	57	35	46	18	47	31	14	37	52	26	51	41

Third parties found virtually no support among students questioned at the time of the first *ER* survey, when faith in our present two-party system was still quite strong on the campuses. At that time, the following results were received:

Check which of the following four attitudes most nearly corresponds to your own?

1) The present two-party system is satisfactory on the whole and should be essentially retained
2) The present party structure should be altered so that much sharper lines could be drawn between the two political parties, one being definitely and unambiguously the more conservative, and the other being definitely and unambiguously the more radical

3) I would support the founding of a third party that would represent "the right" more than either the Republicans or Democrats do at present

4) I would support the founding of a third party that would represent "the left" more than either the Republicans or Democrats do at present

	SL %	Wms %	Yale %	Marq %	BU %	Ind %	SC %	Hwd %	Reed %	Dav %	Bran %	Stan %
1)	40	48	67	77	56	68	59	64	45	66	51	64
2)	27	41	24	14	26	19	25	16	25	24	35	23
3)	4	3	3	3	5	5	9	5		4		4
4)	22	5	2	1	8	3	1	8	17	2	11	4

We are not alone in noting the trend to the left among university students. Our findings in this area correspond to those of Dr. George Gallup, whose American Institute of Public Opinion conducted a nationwide poll of 55 institutions of higher learning between April 23 and May 17 of 1970. Gallup was able to find only two students out of 100 willing to describe their political views as "extremely conservative." He divided his sample into three categories—*All Students, Demonstrators,* and *Non-Demonstrators*—and received the following results:

	All Students	Demonstrators	Non-Demonstrators
Extremely Conservative	2%	2%	2%
Moderately Conservative	19%	10%	22%
Middle of the Road	24%	12%	29%
Moderately Liberal	41%	48%	39%
Extremely Liberal	12%	25%	6%
No Opinion	2%	3%	2%

Gallup also found that party labels no longer seemed to carry the kind of weight they once did. Out of every 100 students questioned by Gallup, only 23 called themselves Republican, while 33 called themselves Democrat, and a whopping 44 called themselves Independent.

V

The rhetoric of the far left has made great strides among our university students since the first *ER* survey. There is a chilling tendency to see things in extreme terms. A majority of students polled view American society as being too repressive, complacent, racist, and sick.

In your opinion, which of the following terms accurately describe American society? (Please check all appropriate responses.)

1) Too repressive
2) Too permissive
3) Too complacent
4) Racist
5) Sick

	SL %	Wms %	Yale %	Marq %	BU %	Ind %	SC %	Hwd %	Reed %	Dav %	Bran %	Stan %
1)	51	42	48	20	38	32	26	36	63	35	56	43
2)	14	10	16	17	4	12	20	13	15	13	7	12
3)	70	63	62	65	52	65	61	35	57	64	64	66
4)	58	44	49	27	41	34	27	71	62	33	51	52
5)	55	37	43	25	50	26	27	55	55	25	52	38

An overwhelming majority of those questioned were sympathetic with the black power movement and its goals, including such programs as black studies, which they considered to be beneficial to black students.

Do you consider the black power movement to be an appropriate response to the condition of the black person in America today?

1) Yes   2) No   3) Unsure or no opinion

	SL %	Wms %	Yale %	Marq %	BU %	Ind %	SC %	Hwd %	Reed %	Dav %	Bran %	Stan %
1)	79	70	64	47	65	46	40	75	77	55	65	65
2)	11	13	19	33	17	33	36	10	8	27	17	22
3)	9	16	14	20	14	18	22	12	13	16	16	13

In your opinion, are the separate and autonomous black studies programs now being established at some colleges and universities academically legitimate?

1) Yes   2) No   3) Unsure or no opinion

	SL	Wms	Yale	Marq	BU	Ind	SC	Hwd	Reed	Dav	Bran	Stan
	%	%	%	%	%	%	%	%	%	%	%	%
1)	54	64	62	49	44	53	35	69	57	46	59	60
2)	26	18	21	25	28	21	33	15	23	26	22	19
3)	16	17	14	25	25	23	30	13	17	26	17	21

Do you think these programs benefit black students?

1) Yes   2) No   3) Unsure or no opinion

	SL	Wms	Yale	Marq	BU	Ind	SC	Hwd	Reed	Dav	Bran	Stan
	%	%	%	%	%	%	%	%	%	%	%	%
1)	57	63	51	42	47	46	35	76	61	45	58	59
2)	16	13	19	24	21	17	30	11	10	15	16	14
3)	25	24	27	33	27	34	33	12	26	37	24	26

At the same time the majority of those polled came out for preferential treatment for blacks in university admissions policy, which they view as a good bargain for society in the long run. Marquette and South Carolina were the only schools where any substantial amount of doubt about the wisdom of such policies was apparent.

In your opinion, is it fair for college admissions offices to give preferential consideration to black applicants?

1) Yes   2) No   3) Unsure or no opinion

	SL	Wms	Yale	Marq	BU	Ind	SC	Hwd	Reed	Dav	Bran	Stan
	%	%	%	%	%	%	%	%	%	%	%	%
1)	59	63	60	23	33	27	14	63	57	46	53	65
2)	25	26	26	69	52	61	80	26	23	43	29	20
3)	14	10	11	8	11	9	5	9	17	8	16	14

Do you think that preferential standards for blacks destroy academic excellence?

1) Yes   2) No   3) Unsure or no opinion

	SL	Wms	Yale	Marq	BU	Ind	SC	Hwd	Reed	Dav	Bran	Stan
	%	%	%	%	%	%	%	%	%	%	%	%
1)	21	23	19	39	27	35	50	14	20	28	28	13
2)	63	55	62	44	50	46	29	76	59	52	52	74
3)	14	20	17	16	20	15	19	8	19	18	18	13

Are such standards of long-term benefit to American race relations?

1) Yes   2) No   3) Unsure or no opinion

74

	SL %	Wms %	Yale %	Marq %	BU %	Ind %	SC %	Hwd %	Reed %	Dav %	Bran %	Stan %
1)	53	64	59	31	40	35	21	51	52	53	49	64
2)	26	16	19	43	31	35	50	16	18	19	19	12
3)	17	19	18	24	24	25	26	29	25	26	29	23

All things considered, do you think more lenient college admissions standards for black applicants should be adopted?

1) Yes   2) No   3) Unsure or no opinion

	SL %	Wms %	Yale %	Marq %	BU %	Ind %	SC %	Hwd %	Reed %	Dav %	Bran %	Stan %
1)	59	61	55	36	42	38	24	63	50	54	62	63
2)	26	24	25	48	38	45	65	24	22	35	22	20
3)	11	11	17	15	15	12	9	9	23	9	13	17

On the question of racial integration, most of those questioned believed it to be both possible and potentially good for our society as a whole. The greatest doubts surprisingly came from predominantly black Howard, where 39 percent of those polled did not consider integration to be possible in America, and where 33 percent did not consider it to be desirable. In contrast to Howard, 70 percent of those polled at South Carolina considered integration to be desirable, and 72 percent considered it to be possible.

Do you believe that integration in the United States is possible?

1) Yes   2) No   3) Unsure or no opinion

	SL %	Wms %	Yale %	Marq %	BU %	Ind %	SC %	Hwd %	Reed %	Dav %	Bran %	Stan %
1)	61	64	56	78	61	67	72	43	59	76	61	61
2)	9	14	22	9	21	16	16	39	17	10	14	16
3)	25	21	19	12	14	15	10	16	22	12	23	22

Do you believe that integration in the United States is desirable?

1) Yes   2) No   3) Unsure or no opinion

	SL %	Wms %	Yale %	Marq %	BU %	Ind %	SC %	Hwd %	Reed %	Dav %	Bran %	Stan %
1)	84	78	77	84	82	80	70	49	87	86	84	82
2)	3	8	11	9	6	11	17	33	2	5	3	3
3)	9	14	9	6	7	7	11	16	8	7	10	14

All indications seem to point to the fact that American students, including students from the South, accept the original goals of the civil rights movement. But there seem to be ominous doubts among the rising black middle class, which, under pressure from black militants, seems to be moving away from those goals. In the future, the pressure for segregated campus housing and segregated classes will come from the blacks. Several American universities have already given in to such pressure.

VI

We found several flagrant examples of what Sir Arnold Lunn has called "selective indignation." Virtually none of those questioned thought that the Soviet Union should be barred from international athletic competition, while a slight majority favored the banning of South Africa from such events.

Do you think the Soviet Union should be barred from international athletic competition?

1) Yes   2) No   3) No opinion

	SL %	Wms %	Yale %	Marq %	BU %	Ind %	SC %	Hwd %	Reed %	Dav %	Bran %	Stan %
1)	3	1	4	2	2	4	4	2			2	1
2)	95	94	92	93	91	89	92	94	94	96	91	96
3)	1	3	2	5	4	4	2	3	3	1	5	2

Do you think South Africa should be barred from international athletic competition?

1) Yes   2) No   3) No opinion

	SL %	Wms %	Yale %	Marq %	BU %	Ind %	SC %	Hwd %	Reed %	Dav %	Bran %	Stan %
1)	54	51	50	29	44	27	25	65	42	34	56	46
2)	32	34	40	59	45	59	65	29	39	56	33	45
3)	12	13	7	11	7	11	9	4	15	9	9	8

The same kind of selectivity was voiced in regard to American intervention abroad. Virtually none of those questioned thought that we were right to intervene in the Dominican Republic, while a slight majority favored intervention in the Middle East if Israel were invaded by a foreign power.

76

If Israel were to be attacked or invaded, which of the following courses of action would you most favor for the United States? (Please check only one response.)

1) Absolute noninterference
2) Aid to Israel short of committing American military forces
3) Aid to Israel including the commitment of American military forces, if forces are requested by Israel
4) Unsure or no opinion

	SL %	Wms %	Yale %	Marq %	BU %	Ind %	SC %	Hwd %	Reed %	Dav %	Bran %	Stan %
1)	38	26	26	38	36	39	24	57	39	32	15	41
2)	36	59	49	39	38	43	57	22	34	56	53	39
3)	5	4	8	9	10	6	12	4	8	4	21	6
4)	17	8	13	12	10	9	4	14	14	6	8	12

There was an equally noteworthy disparity on questions concerning the right of Communist and fascist-styled party members to teach citizenship in public schools. While those polled were all against banning teachers for ideological reasons, an overwhelming majority opposed banning Communists, while a considerable minority favored banning fascists. Double standards, of course, are nothing new in American life. However, it is important to note, from the standpoint of our present study, the kind of ideological prejudices that seem to be dominating our present generation of students: they are distinctly left wing, and in some cases (such as the desire to ban South Africa from international athletic competition) they bespeak a profound lack of critical fairness, which is odd, considering that students attend universities in order, in part, to sharpen their critical faculties. From a conservative point of view, too many of our current crop of students seem to have chosen the wrong side on a number of significant litmus-test issues.

VII

University lectures and contacts are not the only means for conveying political information. We were particularly interested in examining some of the other sources from which the students participating in our survey obtained the facts and opinions upon which they constructed their political beliefs. Interestingly enough, most of those polled claimed that they got most of their information from newspapers, with magazines coming in second, slightly ahead of television, which came in a surprising third.

On which of the following do you most depend for political news, information, and comment? (Please check only one response.)

1) Television
2) Radio
3) Newspapers
4) Magazines

	SL	Wms	Yale	Marq	BU	Ind	SC	Hwd	Reed	Dav	Bran	Stan
	%	%	%	%	%	%	%	%	%	%	%	%
1)	7	11	11	33	20	24	35	24	10	18	16	10
2)	17	1	4	12	13	11	10	10	3	11	11
3)	57	56	63	24	44	35	31	41	35	46	56	48
4)	18	29	19	31	20	25	20	18	33	28	13	27

Here the students differ from their parents, who, according to all reliable data, obtain most of their political information from television.

We asked our participating students to list their main printed sources of political news and comment, and once again we noted the strong tendency to the left (here defined as ranging from the liberal *New York Times* to such far-out publications as *Ramparts*). At four of the Eastern universities (Brandeis, Williams, Sarah Lawrence, and Yale) the *New York Times* dominated the field. At other institutions the major newsmagazines and the local newspapers ran strongly. The conservative *National Review* was at the bottom, while the *Nation*–or–*New Republic* category ran strongly at Sarah Lawrence, Yale, and Reed. *Ramparts* had a particularly significant following at Sarah Lawrence, Howard, and Reed.

Which of the below are your main regular printed sources of political news, information and comment? (Please check all appropriate responses.)

78

1) *Time*
2) *Newsweek*
3) *US News & World Report*
4) *Life*
5) *Ramparts*
6) *National Review*
7) *Nation* or *New Republic*
8) *New York Times*
9) Your college newspaper
10) Your local newspaper
11) Other

	SL	Wms	Yale	Marq	BU	Ind	SC	Hwd	Reed	Dav	Bran	Stan
	%	%	%	%	%	%	%	%	%	%	%	%
1)	49	67	62	70	61	60	56	54	43	62	41	66
2)	41	69	44	43	48	50	49	51	39	65	48	47
3)	5	9	9	18	7	15	22	16	5	20	3	7
4)	14	23	14	26	25	25	29	36	8	37	15	14
5)	14	5	5	3	5	5	2	13	17	6	8	9
6)	3	5	4	3	2	4	6	4	3	7	1	3
7)	18	8	13	3	9	8	7	7	17	8	11	8
8)	86	87	81	7	51	10	12	31	18	10	72	14
9)	33	32	54	39	59	63	58	43	19	40	31	75
10)	12	13	17	73	62	58	80	72	63	80	39	68
11)	38	24	20	23	21	26	29	32	43	22	16	20

VIII

On the religious front, the trend towards secularism continues apace. There is a penchant for the social gospel and theological relativism that has become more pronounced since the first *ER* survey. From the data collected in our current survey, there are strong indications that this phenomenon is at least partially the result of exposure to the contemporary university. A significant minority of those polled noted that their religious practice at university differed from their practice at home. Most of those who admitted to differences in their practice of religion at university, attended services less at college than they did at home, and tended to think more about religion at college than they did at home.

Does your practice of religion at college differ from your practice of religion at home?

1) Yes   2) No

	SL	Wms	Yale	Marq	BU	Ind	SC	Hwd	Reed	Dav	Bran	Stan
	%	%	%	%	%	%	%	%	%	%	%	%
1)	32	37	40	44	24	35	35	26	18	54	26	27
2)	66	63	60	56	76	63	63	72	78	42	71	68

If so, which of the following are aspects of this difference? (Please check all appropriate responses.) (If your practice of religion at college does *not* differ from your practice of religion at home, please skip to next question.)

1) I attend services more regularly at college
2) I attend services more regularly at home
3) I read more about religion at college
4) I am more generally observant at college
5) I am more generally observant at home
6) I think more about religion at college
7) I think more about religion at home

	SL	Wms	Yale	Marq	BU	Ind	SC	Hwd	Reed	Dav	Bran	Stan
	%	%	%	%	%	%	%	%	%	%	%	%
1)	4	5	15	5	6	8	8	10	3	4	6	11
2)	63	83	77	70	67	79	78	79	66	91	70	71
3)	38	39	29	40	20	38	18	24	34	57	19	33
4)	21	8	18	17	13	24	18	24	14	20	4	15
5)	25	14	18	19	38	25	19	21	10	14	49	16
6)	42	39	23	49	31	41	29	28	28	40	43	36
7)	17	5	6	11	11	13	12	24	7	9	15	2

At the time of the first *ER* survey a large number of those questioned thought that religion on the whole stood for the best in human life, and rejected the proposition that religion could be a harmful or an unwholesome influence. At the time we received the following results:

Below are four very brief, rough statements of various attitudes toward "the Church," that is, toward religion. Check the one that most nearly approximates your views:

1) The Church is the one sure and infallible foundation of civilized life. Every member of society ought to be educated in it and required to support it.
2) On the whole, the Church stands for the best in human life, although certain minor errors and shortcomings are necessarily apparent in it, as in all human institutions.

3) While the intentions of most individual Church members are no doubt good, the total influence of the Church may be on the whole harmful. I do not feel I can give it my active support.
4) The Church is a stronghold of much that is unwholesome and dangerous to human welfare. As far as I am concerned, the sooner it declines, the better.

	SL %	Wms %	Yale %	Marq %	BU %	Ind %	SC %	Hwd %	Reed %	Dav %	Bran %	Stan %
1)	4	6	3	61	5	10	8	9			1	7
2)	50	67	73	33	62	74	81	75	40	84	42	64
3)	13	19	15	1	20	8	6	9	34	10	30	20
4)	4	3	2		4	2		2	14	4	16	2

This time around a large number of those polled felt that religion might in fact be an unwholesome and even a harmful influence. Religion seems to have its strongest defenders at Catholic universities like Marquette, and its harshest critics at progressive institutions like Reed and Brandeis.

Below are four very brief, rough statements of various attitudes toward "the Church," that is, toward organized religion. Check the one that most nearly approximates your views.

1) The Church is the one sure and infallible foundation of civilized life. Every member of society ought to be educated in it and required to support it.
2) On the whole, the Church stands for the best in human life, although certain minor errors and shortcomings are necessarily apparent in it, as in all human institutions.
3) While the intentions of most individual Church members are no doubt good, the total influence of the Church may on the whole be harmful. I cannot give it my active support.
4) The Church is a stronghold of much that is unwholesome and dangerous to human welfare. As far as I am concerned, the sooner it declines, the better.

	Sl %	Wms %	Yale %	Marq %	BU %	Ind %	SC %	Hwd %	Reed %	Dav %	Bran %	Stan %
1)			1	1		2	4	2	1	1		
2)	24	36	39	66	36	56	63	54	13	51	25	39
3)	43	43	37	25	42	27	23	29	49	36	42	41
4)	21	14	17	4	16	9	6	9	29	9	26	16

An interesting concomitant of all this is a trend toward religious toleration, which, in a very real sense, reflects growing secularism. At the time of the first *ER* survey, a substantial majority of students voiced opposition to the election of an atheist or agnostic to the Presidency. This time, the number of those so opposed dropped sharply.

Do you have any objection to the election as President of the United States of (please check all appropriate responses):

1) A Roman Catholic?
2) A Jew?
3) A Protestant?
4) An atheist or agnostic?

	SL	Wms	Yale	Marq	BU	Ind	SC	Hwd	Reed	Dav	Bran	Stan
	%	%	%	%	%	%	%	%	%	%	%	%
1)		1	4	1	3	1		4	2	2	2	2
2)		2	6	2	3	4	5	13	3	3	2	3
3)			3	2	1	3		2	1	2	3	1
4)	1	3	14	25	7	30	39	25	3	18	2	5

The one interesting note in this table concerns the 13 percent of Howard students opposed to the election of a Jew to the Presidency, a fact that reflects the subdued but growing level of anti-Semitism that sociologists have observed in the black community. This fact was further emphasized when we asked students if they would have any objections to a member of the same religious grouping being appointed to the presidency of their college. The only strong objection came from Howard: 16 percent of those polled noted that they would object to a Jew receiving that appointment.

Objections to marrying outside the religion of one's birth have also lessened since the time of the first *ER* survey, when we received the following responses to a question on this subject:

Would you have any objections to marrying:

1) A Roman Catholic?
2) A Protestant?
3) A Reform Jew?
4) An Orthodox Jew?
5) An atheist or agnostic?

	SL	Wms	Yale	Marq	BU	Ind	SC	Hwd	Reed	Dav	Bran	Stan
	%	%	%	%	%	%	%	%	%	%	%	%
1)	54	60	53	4	55	53	51	27	57	72	58	45
2)	13	8	7	68	22	10	3	6	17		33	10
3)	9	34	30	77	19	44	50	16	8	54	2	36
4)	54	60	52	80	39	63	72	32	28	70	27	53
5)	13	24	28	88	34	60	66	47	5	52	17	33

Our latest findings indicate that strong opposition to marrying a person of another faith remains only among the religiously orthodox. One of the more interesting findings in this area was the opposition to marrying a member of the Orthodox Jewish community among students at Brandeis.

Would you have any objection to marrying (please check all appropriate responses):

1) A Roman Catholic?
2) An Orthodox Jew?
3) A Reform Jew?
4) A Protestant?
5) An atheist or agnostic?

	SL	Wms	Yale	Marq	BU	Ind	SC	Hwd	Reed	Dav	Bran	Stan
	%	%	%	%	%	%	%	%	%	%	%	%
1)	39	18	23	2	33	18	20	23	31	32	44	24
2)	46	27	38	31	35	34	35	40	32	45	29	35
3)	8	9	19	21	10	24	28	33	15	30	8	17
4)	9	4	11	9	13	5	3	6	14	5	24	9
5)	7	12	20	46	19	35	45	29	6	26	12	17

Religion appears to be a dying force on our nation's campuses, in much the same way that left-wing ideologies appear to be a rising force. Indeed, the growing secularism seems to be only a reflection of the trend to the left, and the corresponding rejection of traditional American values.

IX

Our findings indicate that our young people are wanting in what used to be called "moral fiber." This may simply be a manifestation of the trend to the left, or it may be a reflection of a far deeper civilizational crisis. The so-called drug culture, which is lionized in pop music and mod-films, has made disturbing inroads into the university milieu. Not only did most of the students polled favor the legalization of marijuana, but most of them actually smoked it. Howard, Marquette, Indiana, and South Carolina were the only institutions where strong opposition to the legalization of marijuana was voiced. LSD, on the other hand, does not seem to have caught on, although more than 10 percent of those questioned at Sarah Lawrence, Williams, Yale, Boston University, Reed, and Stanford had used it.

We asked our participating students to indicate their views on drugs by writing the number signifying the following: 1) Definitely in favor; 2) Somewhat in favor; 3) Indifferent or no opinion; 4) Somewhat opposed; 5) Definitely opposed. We received the following results:

Legalization of marijuana

	SL	Wms	Yale	Marq	BU	Ind	SC	Hwd	Reed	Dav	Bran	Stan
	%	%	%	%	%	%	%	%	%	%	%	%
1)	55	48	59	26	54	33	26	22	64	40	56	48
2)	30	28	20	28	26	21	23	23	19	24	24	23
3)	1	9	10	11	6	8	12	14	7	9	5	8
4)	4	9	4	13	7	13	11	6	3	15	5	7
5)	5	6	6	18	6	20	26	23	1	10	5	7

Have you ever smoked marijuana? (Please check one response.)

1) Yes   2) No

	SL	Wms	Yale	Marq	BU	Ind	SC	Hwd	Reed	Dav	Bran	Stan
	%	%	%	%	%	%	%	%	%	%	%	%
1)	82	75	65	33	74	42	34	40	76	33	65	66
2)	18	24	34	67	25	58	65	56	22	66	33	33

Have you ever taken LSD?

1) Yes   2) No

	SL	Wms	Yale	Marq	BU	Ind	SC	Hwd	Reed	Dav	Bran	Stan
	%	%	%	%	%	%	%	%	%	%	%	%
1)	13	18	11	4	18	10	5	1	34	5	8	11
2)	87	82	88	96	81	90	94	96	64	94	91	87

While it is important to make differentiations between drug users and those who would legalize the use of drugs, it must be remembered that the drug culture is not simply based upon the use or advocacy of drugs. It is a lifestyle that may very well lead to the use of various types of drugs, but it can also be a way of acting and talking. Whatever the case, the drug culture, in all its varied forms, seems to have become, at least for the time being, a big thing among the affluent youth of America.

X

The free enterprise system, the cornerstone of America's greatness, seems to have fallen out of favor with the present generation of university students. Socialist and welfarist concepts have become far more attractive to our current crop of students than they were to those participating in the first *ER* survey. Socialism, like dope, has ceased to be a dirty word among the youth of America. A substantial number of those polled were either definitely or somewhat in favor of socialized industries, medicine, and related programs.

Indicate your views on the following political proposals for the United States by writing in a number signifying the following:

1) Definitely in favor
2) Somewhat in favor
3) Indifferent or no opinion
4) Somewhat opposed
5) Definitely opposed

Full socialization of all industries

	SL %	Wms %	Yale %	Marq %	BU %	Ind %	SC %	Hwd %	Reed %	Dav %	Bran %	Stan %
1)	11	2	8	2	9	4		10	11	4	7	3
2)	34	13	17	9	29	14	8	26	27	11	30	17
3)	9	7	11	11	11	9	11	18	16	8	8	7
4)	21	28	25	21	20	20	18	16	14	25	26	23
5)	24	49	40	56	29	51	61	25	29	51	23	48

Socialization of basic industries

	SL %	Wms %	Yale %	Marq %	BU %	Ind %	SC %	Hwd %	Reed %	Dav %	Bran %	Stan %
1)	34	10	21	9	26	13	4	31	29	12	25	15
2)	41	29	34	23	34	20	24	27	28	23	34	29
3)	8	8	6	10	9	8	12	13	11	5	8	8
4)	5	28	22	26	15	22	20	15	13	31	17	22
5)	9	26	17	32	13	34	40	9	16	28	11	24

National health insurance

	SL %	Wms %	Yale %	Marq %	BU %	Ind %	SC %	Hwd %	Reed %	Dav %	Bran %	Stan %
1)	63	39	54	28	56	30	31	54	58	27	61	32
2)	18	35	28	35	27	28	34	25	18	46	22	38
3)	14	14	13	15	11	20	15	14	10	11	9	15
4)	3	6	3	13	3	10	12	3	8	9	1	7
5)		5	2	8	1	8	7		3	5	2	4

Continued governmental projects on the order of the TVA

	SL %	Wms %	Yale %	Marq %	BU %	Ind %	SC %	Hwd %	Reed %	Dav %	Bran %	Stan %
1)	50	27	33	36	41	33	35	30	25	31	34	17
2)	24	43	40	37	27	33	34	21	31	39	26	32
3)	14	18	19	17	21	20	19	39	26	11	27	30
4)	5	8	2	7	5	9	9	4	10	11	4	17
5)	4	4	6	2	4	3	3	2	4	7	1	2

Federal financial aid for cultural activities to the extent of maintaining tax-supported opera, ballet, repertory theaters, orchestras, galleries, poetry fellowships, etc.

	SL %	Wms %	Yale %	Marq %	BU %	Ind %	SC %	Hwd %	Reed %	Dav %	Bran %	Stan %
1)	54	31	40	19	42	19	14	25	39	24	33	24
2)	28	36	32	33	28	28	30	23	29	30	36	33
3)	5	11	13	16	9	16	12	21	8	12	8	18
4)	8	11	10	15	8	20	20	16	10	18	14	11
5)	4	9	5	15	11	15	24	8	10	14	3	10

Establishment of national minimum welfare payment standards

	SL %	Wms %	Yale %	Marq %	BU %	Ind %	SC %	Hwd %	Reed %	Dav %	Bran %	Stan %
1)	55	48	56	42	53	37	28	57	58	39	51	45
2)	29	37	29	33	27	33	33	22	22	36	27	30
3)	7	9	8	7	6	7	15	4	6	10	7	13
4)	4	3	3	9	6	13	14	4	5	9	6	7
5)	3	3	2	8	5	9	10	4	3	5	4	2

If such social and economic views prevail in the years to come, it is clear that America will be mightily changed. The kind of social and economic attitudes that are drummed into our students' heads at university today are the selfsame attitudes that Hayek warned against in *The Road to Serfdom.* That road, it must be remembered, has been trod in our own day by other western nations, nations which were once great, but which today are weak and insignificant.

XI

Most disturbing of all our findings were the defeatist views expressed on the conduct of U.S. foreign policy. We asked our participating students to give their views on the following crucial foreign policy issues by writing the number signifying the following: 1) Definitely in favor; 2) Somewhat in favor; 3) Indifferent or no opinion; 4) Somewhat opposed; 5) Definitely opposed.

Recognition of Red China and support for its admission into the United Nations*

	SL %	Wms %	Yale %	Marq %	BU %	Ind %	SC %	Hwd %	Reed %	Dav %	Bran %	Stan %
1)	57	57	52	24	52	33	19	33	69	34	49	50
2)	26	29	22	30	19	23	23	25	19	30	27	30
3)	11	6	9	13	12	11	13	14	5	11	8	9
4)	3	5	7	12	9	17	14	8	1	15	7	5
5)	3	1	10	20	6	14	31	13	2	9	3	2

Funding of weapons research, development and production necessary to maintain strategic nuclear superiority over China and the Soviet Union

	SL %	Wms %	Yale %	Marq %	BU %	Ind %	SC %	Hwd %	Reed %	Dav %	Bran %	Stan %
1)	4	3	10	10	7	10	21	4	3	6	5	3
2)	4	11	8	24	11	23	38	15	6	21	9	10
3)	4	3	6	5	6	9	7	12	3	9	3	6
4)	17	36	33	34	27	29	22	34	20	31	24	22
5)	68	47	42	25	48	27	12	29	65	33	54	55

These left-wing views were further personified when we confronted our participating students with several crucial litmus-test issues.

Which of the following courses of action would you most favor for the United States with regard to the Ian Smith government in Rhodesia? (Please check only one response.)

1) Absolute noninterference
2) Full support for United Nations economic sanctions designed

*Red China, popularly referred to as the People's Republic of China, has gained admission into the UN since our poll was completed.

to topple the Smith government, but no further action
3) Support in the United Nations for an international military force to bring down the Smith government, should economic sanctions fail
4) Active unilateral support for rebel elements now fighting the Smith government
5) Unsure or no opinion

	SL	Wms	Yale	Marq	BU	Ind	SC	Hwd	Reed	Dav	Bran	Stan
	%	%	%	%		%	%	%	%	%	%	%
1)	14	21	16	23	17	28	23	26	16	24	11	18
2)	53	48	47	29	28	23	26	21	40	44	37	46
3)	9	11	12	6	11	5	6	20	13	7	16	7
4)	3	3	5	1	6	3	2	13	11	1	9	4
5)	16	17	15	39	32	37	41	17	15	22	25	22

Which of the following terms and phrases best describes what you would advocate for American foreign policy? (Please check only one response.)

1) Unilateral disarmament
2) Isolationism
3) Rollback of Communist power
4) Coexistence
5) Containment

	SL	Wms	Yale	Marq	BU	Ind	SC	Hwd	Reed	Dav	Bran	Stan
	%	%	%		%	%	%	%	%	%	%	%
1)	30	19	22	16	27	18	9	19	36	18	26	30
2)		2	2	2	5	3	5	8	3	3	3	2
3)	1	1	2	5	1	3	8	4		3	1	
4)	54	74	62	68	61	62	62	57	53	66	62	61
5)	4	3	5	6	2	10	11	5	3	7	2	3

Which of the following best describes what you would favor for American policy in Vietnam? (Please check only one response.)

1) Escalation in pursuit of victory
2) A limited effort in search of a compromise peace
3) A negotiated withdrawal and a coalition government with the National Liberation Front
4) Immediate withdrawal

	SL	Wms	Yale	Marq	BU	Ind	SC	Hwd	Reed	Dav	Bran	Stan
	%	%	%	%	%	%	%	%	%	%	%	%
1)		1	3	7	4	8	22	3	1	4	2	1
2)	3	8	7	15	6	13	15	4	3	12	4	9
3)	36	44	46	48	30	38	35	29	34	46	22	50
4)	58	46	41	26	56	36	25	59	59	34	71	39

The move to the left in the area of foreign policy undoubtedly has much to do with the rise of the anti–Vietnam War movement. It is, nevertheless, in sharp contrast to the kind of patriotic and anti-Communist views expressed by the students taking part in the first *ER* survey. They are the views of a generation that lacks faith both in itself and in the United States.

XII

The depressing results of our survey all point to one central fact: that the American orthodoxy—that is, the "system" within which Americans of both the democratic left and the democratic right have always been willing to work—is being threatened by forces that most Americans do not completely understand. The far left has made major gains on our nation's campuses; our students have taken to ideology; and the traditional standards of our civilization are being assaulted by the very institutions that once existed to preserve those standards.

One of the major consequences of a liberal education today, James Q. Wilson has noted, "is a set of sympathies which lead many, though not all, persons in a university to acquiesce in the uncivil acts of a small minority."[5] Students in our contemporary universities, Wilson explains, are exposed to a wide range of views pertaining to politics, morality, and conduct; cosmopolitanism is stressed; and numerous ideologies and creeds —regardless of how alien they may be to the American orthodoxy—are presented to students as if they were all somehow perfectly legitimate. Our contemporary students "learn from this experience to appreciate the secret worlds and despise the habits of those persons who, before [their exposure to the modern version of the liberal education], were beyond [their] ken or unpalatable to [their] taste."

As a result of all this, Wilson emphasizes, the modern version of the liberal education erodes the foundations of authority and

5. James Q. Wilson, "Liberalism Versus Liberal Education," *Commentary*, vol. 53, no. 6 (June 1972), pp. 50 ff.

legitimacy upon which the institutions that define and defend the orthodox American concept of freedom and liberty stand. The modern liberal education has thus become the adversary of traditional American liberalism.[6] Everything is criticized in the modern university, even the very intellectual, political, and legal practices that produced the freedom to criticize in the first place. "Freedom exists," Wilson concludes, "because there first existed a certain kind of social order maintained and defined by laws, governments, and authority. Freedom cannot exist outside some system of order, yet no system of order is immune from intellectual assault [in our universities today]."

The old American orthodoxy was based on a system of order that defended itself with such Enlightenment concepts as natural rights. Because it was for so long accepted by most Americans, including most American intellectuals and students, it was immune to the kind of eroding criticism that presently afflicts it. Principles that are widely accepted tend to become dogmas, and if the old American principles have been "debunked" by a generation of liberal and radical critics, it is fair to ask whether we have anything with which to replace them. The radical students clearly would replace our old orthodoxy with a new orthodoxy, not unlike the orthodoxy that prevails in, say, the Soviet Union or Cuba. Thoughtful conservatives, on the contrary, would argue that the old American orthodoxy did in fact work, and is thus irreplaceable. The system, they argue, is fundamentally sound, and must be conserved.

Contrary to Marxist theory, the American working class has always been willing to defend the American system. Often inarticulate and poorly organized from a political standpoint, American workers traditionally refused to embrace radicalism. In this century the advocates of radicalism found their strongest allies and disciples in the middle and upper-middle

6. We use the word *liberalism* here in its accurate sense, meaning a philosophy of freedom and liberation.

classes, among university students and graduates. Dissent in America has generally come from the intellectuals. Among the intellectuals, as Seymour Martin Lipset has demonstrated, and as our findings tend to back up, the dissenters have been drawn mainly from the so-called liberal arts disciplines. Student engineers, agriculturists, and accountants have generally been less willing to embrace radicalism. The liberal and radical impulse has, in our time, been generated by liberal professors, teaching liberal arts subjects, on generally liberal campuses.

Today it has become increasingly difficult for, say, conservative students or teachers to articulate their positions with any success on most of our nation's campuses. The American academy, which helped to destroy the old American orthodoxy, has become the bastion of a series of New Leftist orthodoxies. Such aspects of contemporary liberalism as opposition to the Vietnam War, opposition to further defense spending, and the advocacy of such things as busing to integrate schools, have become the new orthodoxies of the academy; they have been dogmatized, and are thus not fit subjects for discussion. As James Q. Wilson has sadly noted: "[The] list of subjects that cannot be publicly discussed [at Harvard] in a free and open forum has grown steadily, and now includes the war in Vietnam, public policy toward urban ghettos, the relationship between intelligence and heredity, and the role of American corporations in certain overseas regimes. . . . To be specific: a spokesman for South Vietnam, a critic of liberal policies towards the ghettos, a scientist who claimed that intelligence is largely inherited, and a corporate executive who denied that his firm was morally responsible for the regime in South Africa have all been harassed and in some cases forcibly denied an opportunity to speak." One could append more examples from other liberal universities to Professor Wilson's list, but that would be superfluous. The point is that it is almost impossible for a student to be exposed to such a climate of opinion without it in some way moving him to the left.

91

Students willing to work within the American system have achieved many things of importance during the past decade, but their activities have been largely overshadowed by the more numerous, and better publicized successes of the resurgent left. Since the new academic orthodoxy values neither our traditional American concept of academic freedom and tolerance, nor our historic belief in standards of behavior, it is hard to imagine how our quality universities will be able to survive. Our findings suggest that we are heading towards an educational disaster of the first magnitude that promises to transform most of our institutions of learning—primary schools, secondary schools, and universities—into mere way stations on the road to some stultifying Brave New World, resplendent with ideology and devoid of true culture. This, at least, is the disheartening premonition one gets from our survey of student opinion. For the time being, however, all we can say is that our students and our universities have moved very far to the left on a whole range of political, moral, and religious issues since the first *ER* survey. And the future seems bleak.

5

Where Have All the Standards Gone?

Standards are imaginary things, and yet it is extremely doubtful if man can live well, either spiritually or physically, without the belief that they are somehow real. Without them society lapses into anarchy and the individual becomes aware of an intolerable disharmony between himself and the universe.

JOSEPH WOOD KRUTCH

Universities and schools that cast away their inheritance not because they have ceased to believe in its value but out of deference to egalitarian pressure are betraying an intellectual trust and becoming parties to the most recent manifestation of *la trahison des clercs.*

JOHN SPARROW
Warden of All Souls College

THE AMERICAN COLLEGE DIPLOMA, WHICH ONCE stood for something, has been cheapened. Many informed educators now question whether the degrees granted by some American colleges and universities have any value, save that they may attest to the fact that their recipients have warmed the seats of a given institution for four years. Despite the weaknesses that have long been inherent in the majority of America's egalitarian-oriented institutions of higher learning, this was not always the case. At one time—when Albert Jay Nock's Old Regime still prevailed—even the most mediocre American colleges had certain minimum requirements and standards, first for admission, later for graduation, which endowed their degrees with a certain amount of stature. It was tacitly supposed in those days that students graduating from American colleges and universities—and I include the one-room Tank Town variety that so appalled Lord Bryce[1]—had been through some sort of an academic mill; that they had perused certain basic classics; and that they had studied hard and been taught a core curriculum of fundamental subjects in the sciences and the humanities. In short, it was presumed that they had been rendered educated men and women by reason of their graduation from an American college or university, regardless of how humble the school in question might have been.

All that has changed in recent years. The average graduate of a contemporary American university can hardly be called educated in even the vaguest sense of the word, and such basic standards as once existed seem to have gone with the wind. Even the sort of educational mediocrity that so chagrined such diverse early critics of American education as Thorstein Veblen, Irving Babbitt, Charles Beard, and Abraham Flexner, begins to look good by modern standards. One fancies that even the most ardent champions of the progressive movement in early twentieth-century American education would be thoroughly embarrassed could they examine the fruits of their own labors.

While American education has never managed to reach the generally high standards of excellence apparent in many other advanced societies, because of our substitution of quantity for quality, the decline in standards over the past two decades has been so rapid and pervasive as to make a mockery of our educational system. Indeed, future historians of American education

1. James Bryce, *The American Commonwealth* (New York, 1891), 2: 549. Describing an American college of the nineteenth century, Bryce wrote: "I remember to have met . . . a college president—I will call him Mr. Johnson— who gave me a long account of his young university, established by public authority. . . . He was an active sanguine man, and in dilating his plans frequently referred to "the Faculty" as doing this or contemplating that. . . . I asked of how many professors the Faculty at present consisted. 'Well,' he answered, '. . . at present it consists of Mrs. Johnson and myself.' "

may sadly dub this period in our educational history the Age of Destandardization. Even if one accepts the fact that the seeds of recent decline in educational standards were planted by well-intentioned reformers in the earliest days of the Republic, their sudden blossoming, often in hideous forms beyond the wildest dreams of their progenitors, has caught even the most perceptive observers of our educational scene by surprise. Who, only a few years ago, could have possibly predicted the proliferation of gut degrees in such nonacademic subjects as hotel management, peace studies, black English, automotive repair and square dancing?[2] It is one thing to evince a cavalier attitude toward academic standards, and quite another to see those standards obliterated and replaced with a form of garbage that is totally alien to the idea of a university.

Yet, wherever one turns, one is confronted with flagrant examples of the education establishment's willingness to surrender standards, usually in the name of some supposedly important social cause. A recent survey, for example, has noted that while grades are rising at colleges and universities across the land, scholastic aptitude scores are falling. At many institutions grades have risen 10 to 12 percent over the past five years, even though there is no evidence to prove that the quality of students has improved. I have personally known professors who have had a policy of never marking a student below B, and some who had separate standards for marking lower-income students and middle-class students. "Grades don't mean anything to me," a colleague once remarked. "If I like a kid, why should I flunk him?" Another colleague, who specialized in black history, once explained to me that he invariably gave his charges As and Bs in order to instill in them a sense of cultural

2. Ferris State College in Big Rapids, Michigan, has recently received a good deal of attention in the national press. Ferris State grants degrees in such subjects as automobile repair and body mechanics, along with a host of other crafts traditionally associated with a trade school education.

pride. "Besides," he confided, "most of their papers are so badly written that I find it easier to give them automatic As than to wade through their prose."

It is often argued by many modern academics—especially by those who liberally hand out As and Bs—that it is no longer possible objectively to evaluate a student's work. The old standards of evaluation, they argue, are no longer valid. Standards that placed great emphasis on hard work, achievement, and intelligence no longer have any meaning in a pluralistic society. "If one of my students writes 'I is proud' instead of 'I am proud' in a paper," my colleague in black history once noted, "I cannot criticize him, because I cannot impose my cultural standards on him. In his world, 'I is proud' is proper usage, and, after all, who am I to judge?" When I suggested to him that he was, by reason of his professional training, very well qualified to judge his student's bad grammar, he laughed and accused me of being a chauvinist. Standards, he explained, must change with the times. If we applied our old standards to, say, the minority groups that are presently swelling our student population, we couldn't even admit them in substantial numbers, let alone graduate them.

Most of the new destandardization has been done in the name of egalitarianism. Our nation's campuses, it is contended, must be democratized, they must be made to reflect new social trends and new power blocs, and not the old academic standards. Hence we have developed new social standards, based on such concepts as "open enrollment," and "automatic graduation." The advocates of this new egalitarian approach to American education have been backed up by the Department of Health Education and Welfare (HEW), which has done everything within its power to insure that American education, particularly at the university level, will meet the goals of the new academic democracy. HEW has ordered all institutions of higher learning to move at once to bring about "statistically adequate representation" of "women and other minority groups" in their faculties and student bodies. Thus, in the future, standards of faculty employment and student admission at many of our universities may, to one degree or another, be based on such academically irrelevant issues as sex and race, and less on our traditional concept of scholarly and intellectual ability. The new professors may not be very good at their subjects, but if they help to bring about adequate statistical representation of a particular minority group, they will have served their purpose. If the new students are academically wanting in the traditional sense, the curriculum can be altered in such a way as to guarantee their eventual graduation.

Perhaps the most obvious recent example of this new egalitarianism gone mad is the City University of New York (CUNY), which initiated a program of open enrollment for all graduates of New York City high schools in 1970. The various component colleges of CUNY differ in quality and size, from the small community colleges scattered about New York's five boroughs, to the once great City College of New York (CCNY). Of all the components going into the makeup of CUNY, City College has suffered the most under the open-enrollment policy. During the twenties and thirties CCNY was one of the most respected liberal arts colleges in America. It provided an excellent education to the bright but impoverished sons and daughters of New York's working class, and was often referred to as the "Proletarian Harvard," because of the quality of its graduates. There was no open enrollment in those days, and those students who managed to pass CCNY's tough admissions requirements had to work very hard to obtain their degrees.

The advent of the open-enrollment policy changed all that. CUNY was to serve a new purpose; it was going to help New York's notorious mayor John V. Lindsay get the troublesome ghetto high school graduates off the streets for four years; it was going to become—although it was never actually put this way —a diploma mill for the academically botched and unfit high school graduates of New York. The Proletarian Harvard was to become the Blackboard Jungle of American higher education. Not only did CUNY offer tuition-free education to all graduates of New York City high schools, but, according to Dr. Geoffrey Wagner, a professor of English at CCNY, it tended to overlook the high school diploma requirement in many cases.[3]

One of the major problems confronting the faculty of CUNY was the illiteracy of the new open-enrollment students. Many of them could hardly read the English language, and in some cases students could not even speak English. New York, it must be remembered, has a large Puerto Rican population, and many of these Puerto Ricans, including graduates of New York's high schools, have trouble with the English language. But the problem of English illiteracy was not only a Puerto Rican problem. According to Professor Wagner: "Colleagues report remedial [English] classes full of Panamanians, Haitians, Trinidadians, people with but the faintest connection with America when they aren't outright illegal aliens, for the news of the [CUNY] bonanza is getting south."[4] Since New York's public high schools rank rather low nationally in terms of reading skills, the illiteracy problem also embraces American students born to the English language.[5]

Faced with such seemingly insurmountable problems, CUNY authorities had several alternative courses open to them. They could follow the lead of other open-enrollment institutions in other states, and flunk out the academic deadwood at the end of the first term; they could transform the City University into a vast remedial institution, a kind of glorified grammar school; or they could offer a series of gut courses in such

3. Geoffrey Wagner, "Open Admissions in N.Y.: Another Great Hoax," *National Review,* June 23, 1972, p. 694.
4. *Ibid.,* p. 694.
5. The latest data on pupil achievements in New York City schools, as of February 1972, show that the percentage of pupils below the national average in reading skills has grown from 54.1 percent in 1965 to 66.2 percent in 1971. Average reading retardation increased from two months at the second grade level to nine months at the sixth grade level, and almost two years in grades seven through nine.

98

subjects as minority studies. The first course was rejected by the authorities on sociological grounds. The expectations of New York's high school graduates had been raised by the promise of a CUNY diploma, and it would be wrong, and possibly dangerous, to deny them their golden opportunity. If CUNY flunked out all the misfits at the end of the first term, minority groups throughout the city would feel betrayed by the system, and they might seek revenge against the system. The entire state of affairs was explained rather cogently in the CUNY faculty organ, *LC Reporter:*

> To keep faith with our promise to these kids—that we'd give them a fair chance to make it in college instead of cynically proving to them that they can't—*we're watering down our standards.* Out of guilt for not teaching them properly, we're keeping them in college artificially.[6] [Italics added]

The second alternative open to CUNY, that of turning the university into a remedial institution, also posed problems to both the faculty and the students. College professors don't as a rule enjoy teaching remedial classes; it is, rightly, thought to be beneath their dignity. The students, for their part, rejected the remedial approach, which they saw as a form of cultural condescension. "Why should we learn the White Man's culture?" a black student asked a professor who was trying to teach him about Shakespeare. Many students argued that *their* "culture" was every bit as valid as "the White Man's culture"; and they demanded that CUNY reflect what they called "the culture of the streets." This opened the way to the third alternative course for CUNY; and, as of this date, the once proud institution seems to be heading in the direction of minority studies. Already there are courses in black English and Spanglish (the hodgepodge of English and Spanish spoken by many of New York's Puerto Ricans), and there has even been sarcastic talk

6. Quoted in Wagner, *op. cit.*, p. 694.

of a special course in black mathematics.[7] Traditional courses in such seemingly safe subjects as the history of western civilization are being altered to place less emphasis on the Middle Ages and Renaissance, and more emphasis on the glories of Africa and Puerto Rico in their respective golden ages.[8] CUNY has chucked most of its standards to the wind, and it is hard to see anyone taking it seriously as an educational institution again.

Of course, CUNY is an extreme example of the kind of destandardization that is presently afflicting American higher education; but it serves to personify the depths to which an institution that has abandoned its standards can sink. To one degree or another, the kind of destandardization that has taken place at CUNY can be seen, in varying forms, in many other American universities, including universities with very good reputations. Even the Ivy League institutions have adopted some of the gut courses that are *de rigueur* for minority-group students at CUNY. Even at Harvard, where the distinguished black political scientist Martin Kilson has waged a continuing battle against the black studies program, black studies, along with other courses devoted to other minority groups, thrive, attracting those students who are more interested in getting easy alphas than in doing the hard work that is necessary in the more serious disciplines.

The rise of dubious programs in minority and ethnic studies is only part of the problem. The destandardization that is pres-

7. Wagner writes: "According to Professor Ralph Kopperman, who heads the remedial math program at CCNY . . . 40 percent of the remedial students fail to receive passing grades for any of the courses they are in. That's close to half. Kopperman states: 'Many students who come in under open admissions have never had any high school math.'" Wagner goes on to note that some of them have studied some business arithmetic, which, of course, is elementary school stuff.
8. Puerto Rican studies, known officially as "Boricua Studies" (after the name which the *independistas* have chosen for Puerto Rico), are now a big thing at CUNY, and at every other New York institution with a substantial number of Boricuans in its student populace.

ently making a mockery of American education manifests itself in other ways: under the guise of innovations, more and more American institutions of higher learning are discarding the traditional liberal arts education in favor of various cultural fads. At Evergreen State College in Olympia, Washington, for example, students and teachers get together to make up their own course of study. In many instances the chosen course of study is the sort of thing that might best be left to students at a vocational school. One group of Evergreen State students recently received credits for helping to set up a municipal park. At Manhattanville College in Purchase, New York, the authorities have abolished traditional formal course requirements and replaced grades with a pass-fail system, in order to "individualize" their educational program. Students at Manhattanville may now receive credit for extracurricular activities, or for their hobbies. "This is the way to encourage them to develop themselves outside and around the formal curriculum," says Manhattanville's reformist dean, Harold C. Cannon.

The destandardization varies from campus to campus. At Oral Roberts University in Tulsa, students can major in faith healing. The Green Bay campus of the University of Wisconsin has, since 1968, devoted its entire academic program to studying the environment, and all courses relate to such problems as pollution and conservation. While many of the courses taught at these destandardized institutions are of value, taken as a whole, they simply do not provide students with a university education in the traditional sense. As Professor Oscar Handlin noted, in a 1972 commencement address at Brooklyn College, "In the 1970s we sentence more of our youth to more years of school than ever before in history . . . [and yet] never have Americans have been so poorly educated." It is clear that the vast majority of students in our destandardized universities would be better off almost anywhere else—working, or in the army, or in some form of vocational school.

101

II

In our desire to educate as many people as possible through the university level, and even beyond, into graduate and professional schools, we have overreached our capabilities. We simply don't have as many students with the proper motivation and the intellectual capacity to profit from a university education; and we cannot continue to bear the financial burden of the kind of university expansion that has taken place in recent years. We have simply built too many colleges and universities, and forced too many ill-prepared students to spend four or more years in their precincts, studying French history and learning Milton, while their talents and interests lie elsewhere. "Why waste a thousand-dollar education on a five-dollar boy?" Dr. Barnard of Columbia is said to have asked an incredulous nineteenth-century parent. Today the cost of a four-year college education is astronomically higher, but it is not at all clear that the average college student is, academically speaking, worth much more than Dr. Barnard's five-dollar boy.

As a result of our pandering to mediocrity we have constructed, at great expense, many institutions of higher learning that never should have been started in the first place. Most of these institutions serve no genuine educational purpose, save, perhaps, temporarily to pound a little culture into unwilling heads. Perhaps the only plausible apologia one can offer for the tank-town colleges and glorified diploma mills that dominate so much of the American university scene is that they keep some of the kids off the streets and out of the job market for four years. But surely we could achieve the same end for far less money without packing so many of our high school graduates into liberal arts colleges.

The proliferation of third-rate colleges, catering to the needs of third-rate students, has led to other problems. The most immediate problem confronting these inferior institutions, along with our serious universities and colleges, is a financial one. We have spread our financial recources too thin. If large sums of private and public money go to third-rate institutions, first-rate institutions, which need and deserve financial aid, must correspondingly get less money. The result is obvious. Today all American universities, from Harvard down to the lowliest diploma mill, are feeling the financial pinch. All this is exacerbated by the fact that money for higher education is scarce today.

A large number of our colleges and universities—especially the inferior ones—are, as a result of these conditions, on the verge of folding. The plight of the endangered institutions has caused a great deal of consternation among educators and public officials, and has led to President Nixon's signing of the new Higher Education Act of 1972. While it is not surprising that educators should be concerned over the fate of those serious institutions presently experiencing financial troubles, it is difficult to comprehend their concern over the fate of the second-rate institutions, which, if they do anything, only drain money away from the hard-pressed institutions that really deserve to survive. At present there are 400 American colleges and universities on the brink of going out of business.[9] The Association of American Colleges (AAC), a group of 554 of some of the smallest and least-important colleges in America, has predicted that about 200 colleges will go broke before the end of 1972, and that some 200 more will fail within the next decade. By the 1980s, the AAC report continues, approximately 40 percent of our large Ph.D.–granting universities will be reduced to hollow

9. William A. Henry III, "The College Money Crisis," *Boston Sunday Globe*, May 28, 1972. Henry, like so many education journalists, displayed a genuine concern over the future of second-rate institutions. He began his article as follows: "Just before Easter vacation this year, the girls of Cardinal Cushing College . . . 'wept hysterically,' in the words of the disconsolate college president, at the news that the debt-ridden school would fold after graduation in May." One wonders, did Cardinal Cushing College, which was little more than a finishing school for middle-class Catholic girls, *really* deserve to survive, especially if its survival would serve only to take money away from a more deserving institution? The answer must be an emphatic no!

shells of their former glory, with nothing more than their football stadiums to attest to what they once were. This, the AAC laments, is inevitable, even if the threatened institutions economize down to the bone, discarding unprofitable programs, selling property, and holding bingo games. The only possible hope for these institutions, the AAC report concludes —reminding us again of the dream of all American university administrators—is a massive and immediate increase in federal aid. Better, they argue, to federalize these institutions than to allow them to go out of business.

If, as the AAC has calculated, 400 American institutions of higher learning are on the verge of going out of business, with many more to follow, it is clear that the federal government's involvement would indeed have to be a massive one. Forgetting, for the moment, the traditional American fear of a nationalized system of higher education, the AAC proposal is a rather hefty burden to foist on the shoulders of the American taxpayer. However, it is more than likely that the long-suffering American taxpayer—with his historic belief in the sanctity of *all* forms of education—will readily assume this added tax burden, even though the 400 threatened colleges and universities do not really deserve to survive. Americans have willingly endured many financial sacrifices in the past in order to provide for our educational system, and it seems unlikely that their overly generous attitude toward education will change in the foreseeable future. The average taxpayer is simply not in the position to evaluate the educational worth of a given enterprise, and so he simply coughs up the needed funds without so much as a whimper of protest.

The new Higher Education Act (HEA), passed by Congress and signed into law by President Nixon in June 1972, will provide up to one billion dollars of tax money each year in institutional aid to our beleaguered colleges and universities. The aid will come in the form of direct grants, which the institutions in question may use as they see fit, a departure from our traditional concept of special-purpose aid.[10] The bill also provides for "emergency grants" to institutions (such as those described above) that are in danger of collapsing. However, there is reason to believe that the emergency grants will be too small and too late to save most of the threatened 400 colleges and universities. "At no time in the foreseeable future," writes Peter Muirhead of the U. S. Bureau of Higher Education, "is Congress likely to appropriate enough money to keep all the . . . colleges in operation." The Carnegie Commission on Higher Education put the matter more succinctly in its report, *The More Effective Use of Resources: An Imperative for Higher Education,* published shortly before the latest federal attempt to rescue our threatened institutions of higher learning. Arguing that federal funds were not the solution to the financial crisis in American higher education, the report emphasized: "It is not enough to bemoan fate or to look to others for help. . . . Higher education must also help itself."

It is clear that we are wasting our resources in trying to rescue the many mediocre colleges that are in danger of going out of business. Since they serve no true educational function they deserve the oblivion for which they are destined. The money spent on these second-rate institutions might be better spent on the serious American colleges and universities that are also in deep financial trouble, where it would do some good. For it must be remembered that even Harvard, our wealthiest private university, with an endowment of over one billion dollars is having serious financial problems. If we forget about the mediocre institutions that do not deserve to survive, and concentrate our efforts on our major institutions, we might begin the process of returning American higher education to the business of educating serious students in serious subjects.

10. Eric Wentworth, "No Silver Spoon for Education," *The Saturday Review of Education,* vol. 55, no. 30, pp. 38, 39. Wentworth notes that while the HEA offers direct grants, threatened institutions will still have to compete for a host of special-purpose clauses contained in legislation.

III

Whether American higher education can ever regain the kind of minimal standards it once possessed is debatable. Certainly in a society where a college degree is considered to be the *sine qua non* to success, it will be difficult to revive standards. The tank-town colleges came about to accommodate those students in our degree-crazed society who couldn't meet the standards of the more serious institutions. As long as we continue to overstress the importance of college certification, mediocre students, who might be better off learning a serious trade, will continue to flock to mediocre institutions, which might serve society better by going out of business.

One would think that the numerous accredited mediocre institutions, which, as we have noted, are nothing more than diploma mills, would make it possible for every American this side of mental retardation to obtain a diploma. But this apparently is not the case. A *New York Times* survey has discovered that unaccredited colleges are on the rise in this country.[11] Of the 3,000 colleges and universities in the United States today, only 2,700 have met the perfunctory standards of accreditation that separate legal diploma mills from illegal diploma mills. The U. S. Office of Education, which does not list the accredited City University of New York as a diploma mill—a fact which reflects upon the Office's typically low standards—lists only 110 of the 300 unaccredited American colleges as diploma mills. The Office of Education narrowly defines a diploma mill as an organization that "awards degrees without requiring courses of instruction that all reputable educational institutions require before conferring degrees." Since most of the unaccredited colleges in America actually offer course instruction over a four-year period, they do not fall into the Office's definition of a

11. M. A. Farber, ". . . Unaccredited Colleges in U. S.," *New York Times*, July 27, 1972, p. 1.

diploma mill. On the other hand, it must be noted, that an accredited institution like CUNY offers some pretty dicey subjects to a student body that may well rank below the intellectual level of the student bodies at many of the unaccredited colleges in America. One wonders what differences in educational value separate a sheepskin purchased from a store-front diploma mill and a *theoretically* earned degree from CUNY under open enrollment? I frankly cannot see that the CUNY degree is any more representative of a true university education than a degree from some fly-by-night diploma mill.

A bona fide diploma mill, in the Office of Education's sense of the term, is a place that offers a quickie degree (usually a doctorate or a law degree) for a fee ranging from only a few dollars to as high as five thousand dollars. Students need not attend classes, read any books, take any examinations. The institutions themselves often consist of nothing more than a post office box or a small office, although in a few rare cases they actually operate small campuses and offer classes in various subjects. Just as the educational standards of various accredited colleges vary sharply, so also do state laws regarding the incorporation of "degree-granting" institutions. It is not surprising, therefore, to discover that states with lax laws in this area, like Florida and California, have become the major havens in this country for diploma mills. In Florida, until very recently, a person could found a degree-granting institution by paying $37 to the state. In California, any organization possessing $50,000 in assets, to be used for educational purposes, can confer college degrees.

The sad fact is that the educational consumer—which is to say, the average citizen—doesn't know where to turn. There is even good reason to believe that educators who ought to know better don't know where to turn. The *New York Times* investigation revealed that educators and psychologists with Ph.D.'s from various unaccredited diploma mills presently hold high-ranking positions on the faculty and in the administration at

107

CUNY and several other accredited New York universities. If one appends to the officially recognized diploma mills the hundreds of unaccredited institutions that are not so recognized, and the thousand or so accredited institutions that really offer little more in the way of an education than the unaccredited schools, one begins to appreciate the extent of the problem confronting the student in search of a genuine education today. It all boils down to the fact that American educators have been so lax about standards for so long a time that they have come to tolerate the existence even of the wretched diploma mills, often citing them as being "innovative" or "experimental."

The fact remains that an earned degree from many of our accredited colleges and universities is often not worth much more than a degree purchased from a diploma mill. We have lowered the undergraduate and postgraduate standards at so many of our accredited institutions that many employers simply write off the graduates of 90 percent of America's colleges and universities, and concentrate their hiring efforts on the graduates of our elite institutions, such as Harvard and Yale. A bright student, having emerged from one of our lesser colleges or universities with his devalued B.A. in hand, will seek out an elite graduate or professional school to make amends for his near worthless undergraduate degree; while his less-gifted fellow students, having also come to recognize that their degrees have declined in value, may fall prey to some diploma mill in a desperate effort to augment their credentials. In a more standardized system of education, the bright student would have been channeled into a good university in the first place, while his less-gifted brothers and sisters would have gone off to master a useful trade.

As standards decline, and as colleges and universities go out of business, many Americans have begun the painful process of reevaluating the goals of American education. To date, American higher education has distinguished itself from, say, European higher education by its instrumentalism. Americans, as Albert Jay Nock noted, traditionally view higher education as a means to earning a living, while Europeans have traditionally viewed it as a preparation for living itself. As early as 1918, Thorstein Veblen criticized American higher education for succumbing to the "businessman mentality." The university boards, administrations, and even the faculties, Veblen lamented, were dominated by this mentality. The boards were controlled, he wrote, by captains of industry, the faculties by captains of erudition.[12] As for the students, they were to be prepared to enter into the business world; and such culture as they picked up along the way would be used to further their business careers.

Yet even if we accept the fact that American higher education has set rather low educational goals for itself, it is fair to ask, in this age of destandardization, whether in fact it is even succeeding in reaching these limited goals, whether it is preparing people for a productive life in the business world. Speaking on the CBS television documentary "Higher Education: Who Needs It," reporter Hughs Rudd noted: "In our pursuit of success, we place an incredible amount of trust in higher education: It's an article of faith in this country that the more education you have, the more money you can make. As a result, the vast machinery of higher education in the United States is behaving like a runaway factory, producing ever-increasing numbers of graduates. . . ." The rewards for all this education,

12. Thorstein Veblen, *The Higher Learning in America* (New York: Kelley, 1918), pp. 68 ff.

Rudd lamented, are a good deal less tangible. "We like a return on the dollar," he explained, ". . . but most of today's graduates are not getting it. We thought, of course, that we were doing the right thing, but, as we're learning more and more these days, the road to hell sometimes is paved with good intentions, and with the best intentions in the world, we've put our young college graduates in one hell of a fix."[13]

Rudd's point was augmented in an editorial published in *Change,* a journal devoted to higher education. "The power of colleges to certify 'success' is already much diminished," the editorial declared. "It would be sublimely silly," *Change* continued, "to warn every entering freshman . . . that a college education 'may be harmful to life.' But it would be equally dishonest to have him believe the bucolic themes of his college catalogs, only to have his encapsulated four-year Garden of Eden end in a nightmare of unemployment lines."[14] Nevertheless, all available data point to the fact that our destandardized colleges and universities have failed in their function as potential placement agencies for the business world. The reason for this failure is very simple: a businessman would have to be mad to employ the graduates of certain institutions of higher learning, especially in a buyers market, when jobs are scarce, and he can take his pick of the best graduates from the best universities. One might also add that the universities have come to this sad situation largely because of the fact that they've endeavored to transform themselves into glorified trade schools in the first place. Universities cannot serve two masters: they cannot exist as employment agencies and educational institutions at the same time; they cannot offer students gut courses and expect them to find jobs easily after graduation. If they are to be universities, they must be universities with serious academic standards: if they are to be trade schools, they

13. Quoted in George W. Bonham's editorial, "Higher Education: Who Needs It?" *Change,* vol. 4, no. 6 (Summer 1972), p. 11.
14. *Ibid.,* p. 12.

must end the pretense of being universities and become good trade schools, also with high standards.

"Higher education," Fritz Machlup, former president of the American Association of University Professors, has noted, "is too high for the average intelligence, much too high for the average interest, and vastly too high for the average patience." Higher education, in the historic sense of the concept, was simply not designed for the average person. It is, by definition, elitist in character, beyond the intellectual capacity of the common man. Nevertheless, American educators have often refused to accept this fact. This is why there are so many colleges and universities, both accredited and unaccredited, in the United States. This is why so many students with average and even below-average intellects are encouraged to go on to college or university. Education, the champions of egalitarianism contend, must be opened to all. We must not have an elitist system of education, for such a system would run counter to the democratic ethos.

In the end, however, everyone suffers. Those with the capacity for higher education are dragged down to the levels of those who lack that capacity. Gifted students must endure the slow pace of education in the average American college or university, so as to allow slower students an *equal* chance. The average college student, who would be better off elsewhere, is forced to spend four years studying subjects that do not prepare him for a productive life, subjects in which he may have no interest whatsoever. In the end, they all graduate together, and they discover that the job market is not as generous as the student market. They have not been educated, since most of them were not educable in the first place. But they also lack the kind of practical skills that will enable them to earn a living.

American universities have succeeded in devaluing the liberal education, only to replace it with an instrumentalism that is too vague to prepare effectively its victims for the real world. While formative education has more or less died, the instru-

111

mentalism that has taken its place is largely of a theoretical sort. Instead of studying, say, Latin poetry, a student can study urban race relations, an instrumental course that will be of little use to him in the real world. While some universities offer degrees in such instrumental subjects as hotel management and accounting, the standards for these courses are so low that the graduates who manage to find work have to be retrained on the job.

V

The alternative to all this is simple. From a very early age students should be segregated according to their intellectual ability. Those students who appear, on the basis of their work and various test scores, to be intellectually inclined, should be sent on to elite grammar and high schools, where they can mingle with other gifted children and concentrate on serious academic work. By the time a student reaches puberty, his teachers should be able to tell whether he is college material or not. If a student has no real interest in academic subjects, he should be directed into job training in some skill in which he seems to be interested. This way vocational training can begin while a student is still in his early teens, preparing him for immediate employment upon graduation. The vocational training, of course, would be very broad, and would undoubtedly cover many areas presently covered in certain universities.

Students wishing to go into more highly skilled careers, say, paramedicine or accounting, would be sent to institutions that specialized in these subjects. The period of their residency might be as long as four years. However, the student bodies at these new institutions would not have to study liberal arts subjects. In most cases they could probably complete their training

112

two years after their graduation from high school. One could envisage transforming many of the 400 colleges that are presently going out of business into advanced technical schools. Of course, there would be no such thing as open enrollment at these institutions. Students would have to demonstrate an aptitude for whatever skill they wished to study.

Liberal education in the arts and sciences would be confined to the graduates of the elite academic high schools. The B.A. would be restored to some semblance of its former value. Universities would cease performing the kind of sociological functions that places such as CUNY presently perform. Their main job would be educational: expanding the frontiers of knowledge, training young scholars, and serving as reservoirs of culture.

While some of these things may seem farfetched at the present moment, there is ample evidence to indicate that many influential educators are coming to realize that our present system of higher education is not working. Open enrollment is recognized by almost every sane educator to be both a farce and a waste of valuable resources. More and more, educators are beginning to favor some form of career education as an alternative to the present mess. We may begin, as a result, to see more institutions like Ferris State College, and fewer places like CUNY. First, of course, the present wave of egalitarian experimentation, which has created such places as modern-day CUNY, will have to be exposed for what it is. This will happen in time. Let us hope that it happens sooner rather than later. The American welfare state cannot afford to absorb many more graduates of ersatz universities like CUNY.

The one fear that remains is that it may be too late for serious academic education in America. Already the classical Latin-Greek education has lapsed into an oblivion from which it will never return. The standards have been so low in so many subjects for so long that, in many cases, it will be difficult to restore

113

them to the kind of health they once enjoyed. It will be a difficult struggle. But if the American college diploma is ever to regain the kind of meaning and value it once possessed, we will have to move fast—before it really is too late.

6

The Federal Schoolmaster

SINCE THE PASSAGE OF THE NATIONAL DEFENSE Education Act (NDEA) in 1958, the federal government has concerned itself increasingly with education. In the deluge of education legislation enacted by the 88th and 89th New Frontier–Great Society Congresses (24 major pieces of legislation) the federal presence became the major fact in American education; the U. S. Office of Education—once a meager statistics-gathering bureaucracy —became one of the most powerful and influential organizations in Washington, disposing of billions of dollars and permeating virtually every sector of American life; and the concept of "local control" of American education became less and less significant for American educators.

One need only recall the crisis-oriented language of the NDEA ("The present *emergency** demands that additional and more adequate educational opportunities be made available . . ."), or Admiral Rickover's widely publicized pontifications on the *failure* of American education to keep pace with the demands of modern science and technology, for examples of the emotional hysteria that prefaced the federalization of American education. What began so innocently with the (Northwest) Ordinance of 1787, which established educational institutions in the Northwest Territory, has culminated in such bills as the Elementary and Secondary Education Act of 1965, which has already begun to transform the American

*Italics added.

115

school to fit the needs of the U. S. Office of Education.

The time may come, notes Mr. Francis Keppel, former U.S. commissioner of education and former assistant secretary for education under Presidents Kennedy and Johnson, when the federal government will control rather than aid American education. In a certain sense that time has already arrived. The prevailing pattern among most professional educators—indeed, among most Americans—is one of spontaneous acquiescence to each new federal demand; and one is hard pressed to find articulate opposition to the ever-increasing power of Washington in the sphere of education. It is presumed that the federal role in education is both good and necessary, and anyone venturing to disagree with this presumption can be easily consigned to the world of Miniver Cheevy. The opponents of the new federal role, it will be reasoned, don't really care about the youth of America.

Whatever the case, the salient fact is that we are presently spending more money on education than we ever have before in our history. Total expenditures (local, state, and federal) for public schools alone have reached over $50 billion a year. The monies spent on education presently amount to roughly 8 percent of a much smaller GNP on education. Education, in Mr. Keppel's words, has become "big busines." The federal share of this massive expenditure is still only a small percentage but it is small percentage with great power for influencing the course of American education. Today, with $16 billion to spend on education, the federal government provides 20 percent of all money spent on elementary and secondary schools. But figures alone, as William K. Stevens has noted, do not tell the whole story. "Washington's influence," he explains, "is far greater than dollar amounts would suggest. Federal tendrils reach into every corner of the educational enterprise." Southern senators, who might be expected to know better, have been known to tremble at the thought of their states losing their 7.5 percent of federal aid for failure to comply with Title VI of the Civil

Rights Act of 1964; and superintendents of wealthy suburban schools, which get a much smaller cut than the rest of the nation, would rather curtail certain educational activities than lose their puny 1 percent; for it is held, as an article of faith, that the federal government can achieve all the various goals that have somehow eluded the states and local communities.

At one time the supporters of massive federal aid to education campaigned under the slogan, "Federal Aid Without Federal Control." That was before the NDEA and the Economic Opportunity Act and the Higher Education Act and the Elementary and Secondary Education Act, to give only a partial list, supplied them with enough muscle to dump their old slogan. The Office of Education has persistently used federal funds as a club with which, for example, to bash those Southern states still wallowing in their segregated sties. When certain knowledgeable political leaders sought to remind the Office of Education that the Tenth Amendment to the Constitution was rather specific about the division of responsibilities between the state and federal governments—hinting that the Office was overstepping its bounds—the full force of the liberal press mobilized to disagree with them.

As long as there is one hint of segregation anywhere in the country, it was argued, the Office of Education must continue to withhold funds. With this kind of rhetoric booming in the land, education has become essentially an instrument of federal policy, and the Office of Education has developed into a kind of sociological police force, determined to equalize *all* American education, whatever the cost in money and suffering.

II

The United States, unlike most European countries, never had a central ministry of education. Education, as Alexis de Tocqueville noted, was in the hands of the various local communities and private groups. This, Tocqueville recognized, was the genius of the American system. Of course, there were those who yearned for central control. At the Constitutional Convention, there was a movement to establish a national university, but it was rejected by our Founding Fathers, and education was not even mentioned in the Constitution. In 1795, George Washington wanted to establish a national university, as did John Quincy Adams later on. A national system of education, it was argued, would grow from such a university, and this would be good for society as a whole. But the various schemes for nationalizing American education never caught on. It was simply not part of the American character to say, as one nineteenth-century French educator is reported to have said, that at any time of the school day he had only to look at his clock to know exactly what every child in France was studying. And while Americans, from the time of the Founding Fathers on, have stressed the importance of education, they have *always* viewed nationalization of the school with great skepticism. Nevertheless, despite our original intentions, the federal government has become the single most potent force in American education, and the Office of Education has virtually become our ministry of education.

A closer examination of the thinking behind the federal role may help to explain the revolution (Francis Keppel has called it the "necessary revolution") that is presently sweeping American education. American educationists, unlike most other Americans, have traditionally been repelled by the heterogeneity that distinguishes American culture; they have long sought to establish what Horace Mann, the father of American educationism, called the "common culture"—that is, a socially and intellectually integrated and egalitarian society. Mann, and later John Dewey, recognized that the school was the best place to achieve this end. Dewey, it should be noted, was more ambiguous about the common culture than many of his disciples. Unlike his more radical followers he viewed gov-

118

ernmental intervention in the realm of education as a corruption of the social ends of education, and when he spoke of equality in education, he meant not an intellectual equality but a moral equality, which implied that all students were entitled, where possible, to the type of schooling that would enable them to do whatever they were intellectually capable of doing. Dewey was not a policy-oriented man, and it is not clear how he expected his proposals to come to fruition without some form of governmental intervention. For Dewey, unlike his disciples (who were to pervert his work), the school was *not* the sociological melting pot of the present day, although he clearly believed that the school was capable of becoming such a melting pot.

Although Dewey was ambiguous, his followers were not. They erected upon his ideas the fundamentals of modern educationism. That the ideology we call Deweyism is a distortion of Dewey's initial philosophy of education is, for our purposes, no longer important. Future historians will eventually set things right. The salient fact remains that John Dewey—even for those who have never managed to wade through his ponderous prose—is used as a theoretical justification for every wretched little thing our educational establishment wishes to foist upon us. The Deweyites dominate American education at all levels, from the little teachers' colleges of the Midwest to the vast federal bureaucracy in Washington.

The egalitarianism of the common culture is, in Professor Lawrence Cremin's phrase, "a proposition that must really be accepted on faith since the whole idea of democratic culture is too new to have stood the test of time." Rarely has the thinking of the liberal educationist been more eloquently exposed— *benignus etiam dandi causam cogitat.* Leaving aside such trite side issues as the universal educability of the species, the fact that Cremin, with one of the best minds among our current crop of educationists, is forced to base his argument on faith rather than experience, only serves to exemplify the kind of

119

banality upon which educationist thinking is built. It is assumed, as an article of faith, that a common, integrated, democratic educational system is both possible and desirable; and that from this egalitarian educational system a common culture, free from the problems that have plagued societies in the past, will emerge. There is in America only one body strong enough to bring this situation into existence—the federal government.

III

Although one can trace the idea of increased federal intervention in education back to the Northwest Ordinance and to the early movement for the establishment of a national university, it did not receive real impetus until its cause was taken up by the progressives in our own century. These men saw that the concept of local control stood in the way of the common culture; there were simply too many differences and too much individuality under our system of local control. The difference between, say, New York's educational system and Alabama's was (and is) too much for these well-meaning reformers to bear. Even a careful examination of New York State, which spends huge sums of money on education, will reveal the kind of inequalities against which good progressives have always recoiled. New York, an educationist's utopia, spends more money on education than any other state ($1,889 for every student attending a public school in 1971), but it does not have an equal distribution of this money. The school district in New York with the highest expenditure per pupil, for example, spends around seven times as much as the district with the lowest.

Former Harvard president James Bryant Conant, perhaps the most influential educational writer in America today, argues along similar lines in his book, *The Comprehensive High School* (New York: McGraw-Hill, 1967). Conant believes

120

that our tradition of local control has created an inequality that can be remedied only by a massive dose of federal intervention. When the federal government eventually steps in to "solve" this problem, he maintains, it will have to go beyond mere equalizing of the amount of money spent on each pupil; for some children—particularly the products of the urban ghettos —will require much more money than the average. In the end, the federal government will have to work out an extremely complex and selective system for allocating "funds-to-make-things-equal," which will probably prove to be as unsuccessful as previous attempts by the federal government to solve the other genuine problems which afflict the poor in America. Social Darwinism is bad, but massive federal spending has proved to be little better.

If education is powerful enough to bring about the reorientation of society foreseen by men like Dr. Conant, it would appear, to a less ideological mind than his, to be a dangerous instrument to place in the hands of the federal government. Indeed, from a very early time, critics of a large federal role in education have argued with John Stuart Mill, that state intervention in the realm of education is nothing more than a "contrivance for moulding people to be exactly like one another." Arguing along similar lines, Professor F. A. von Hayek reminds us that the "very magnitude of the power over men's minds that a highly centralized and government-dominated system of education places in the hands of the authorities ought to make one hesitate before accepting it too readily.... In the field of education perhaps more than any other, the greatest dangers to freedom are likely to come from the development of psychological techniques which may soon give us far greater power than we have ever had to shape men's minds deliberately." It is doubtful that a genuinely moderate man like Dr. Conant would ever advocate molding people to be exactly like one another; yet his passionate desire to make things equal (that is, the same) and his call for massive doses of federal intervention do not bode well for anything even distantly resembling individualism.

The vaunted common culture has yet to be achieved, but there can be little doubt that recent years have brought us much closer to it. As early as 1959, Ronald F. Campbell, in a much publicized work, could speak of the "folklore" of local school control. While it is still possible to talk in terms of limited local control, the federal government has taken a position of immense influence which seems to increase each year. The rapid growth of the National Science Foundation and of the Office of Education; Supreme Court decisions such as *Everson* (1947), *McCollum* (1948), *Zorach* (1952), and *Brown* (1954); and the great wave of federal education legislation enacted by the 88th and 89th Congresses—all these developments have become the weapons of the expanding federal role. With the rise of busing in the 1970s, the real power of the federal government over various local school districts for the first time became apparent to all American citizens.

A close examination of our numerous federal aid to education programs reveals a style of legislation that appears to be bent more on altering the social order in America than on improving our schools and universities. If, for instance, federal funds can be used to eliminate a situation that the Office of Education and its allies consider to be a social evil, so much the better; this is what led Mr. Keppel to prod the Office out of its statistical somnolence in the first place, and transform it into its present position of affluence and power. What is more, the general public—viewing this entire policy as being somehow *beneficial* to learning—seems all too willing to leave things to the ideologues in the Office of Education. After all, Americans have never been stingy when it comes to supporting education. If anything seems likely to shatter the public's faith in the educational bureaucracy, it seems to be busing: but it is still too early to predict how the antibusing movement will affect the rest of the federal role in American education.

But if the general public is only really concerned about bus-

122

ing, others are concerned about other aspects of federal aid legislation. As early as 1967, the National Education Association's Educational Policies Commission attacked the special-purpose categories, such as special programs in reading, foreign languages, and science, that come with all federal aid to education. The commission argued that "special-purpose federal aid . . . is itself a form of government control of education . . . an indirect but nevertheless powerful influence . . . upon what is taught; and the priority of resources, time, and money allocated to it." The commission report further noted that "state and local educational authorities tend to view such [categorical] aid as a conglomeration of projects rather than as fundamental parts of a coherent educational system." But categorical or special-purpose aid is really the only kind of federal aid this country has ever known; it is the only effective way of *using* education as an instrument of federal policy, which is exactly the reason for its existence. To date, our federal aid has always come with categorical strings attached, a fact which the National Education Association (NEA) surely knew in 1964 when it accepted categorical grants "as a means of getting the flow of federal funds established." The NEA rather naively assumed that massive categorical assistance could be converted into general aid which the various states and local communities could spend as they saw fit. It is, after all, difficult for the modern American educationist, with his unflinching faith in the innate power of the federal government to do good, to apprehend the fact that the federal government's motives may be different from his own. Once you ask the state to do something *for* you, Albert Jay Nock once warned, you must also expect the state to do something *to* you. There simply is no such thing as federal aid without federal strings attached to it.

But such doubts and misgivings as have existed about federal strings have not stopped American educators from looking to Washington for help. There are even some educators who would have the federal government assume the major role in American education. Perhaps the only thing standing in the way of a total federal takeover is the concept of categorical aid. If categorical aid were replaced with a program of unrestricted general aid, few American educators would be willing to turn it down. Already there is a movement in this direction in Congress, and President Nixon's commissioner of education, Sidney P. Marland, has said that he favors the federal government paying 25 to 30 percent of the cost of public education. The recent California Supreme Court ruling, in *Serrano* v. *Priest,* which declared the local property tax to be discriminatory, may well be used as a justification for such a program of general aid. Assuming that such a partnership between the federal and state governments were Constitutional, and assuming that the government could get the money to go into education in so big a way, we then could fairly predict the death of local control of American education.

IV

Although it is not possible to chart the exact course on which the federal aid programs will travel in the years to come, it is possible to say some things about how the federal government has influenced American education up to the present day.

We might begin with higher education, an area that has been less exhaustively studied than elementary and secondary education. Here we find many examples of negative federal influence and control. Commenting on this sad situation, Dr. Clark Kerr, the former president of the University of California, observed:

A university's control over its destiny as been substantially reduced. [Federal] funds . . . commit some of the university's own funds; they influence the assignment of space; they determine the distribution of time as between teach-

124

ing and research; to a large extent they establish the areas in which a university grows fastest; almost imperceptibly a university is changed.

Quite often, Kerr notes, a university is placed in the position of either accepting a particular piece of federal aid or losing a faculty member, because, unlike the rest of a university's financial transactions, which must go through the usual budget-making channels, federal funds are usually negotiated for by an individual faculty member and a particular governmental agency. As a result, Kerr continues, "20 to 50 to 80 percent of a university's expenditures may be handled outside of normal channels." Under these conditions the whole authority of the university is reduced. "Some faculty members come to use the pressure of their [federal] agency against their university. They may try to force the establishment of a new administrative unity or assignment of land for their own special building, in defiance of general university policy or priorities." Eventually the university may discover that parts of its faculty have shifted their loyalty from the university to the federal agency handing out aid. The faculty is thus transformed, thanks to well-placed federal grants, into a body of "tenants rather than owners, taking their grants with them as they change universities."

Mr. Gerald Piel, the publisher of *Scientific American*, has taken Dr. Kerr's criticism one step further:

The Federal grant universities have weakened their autonomy and so their capacity to fulfill their function as the corporate agents of free inquiry. They have explicitly surrendered this function to the extent that they have undertaken to serve as the executors of Federal policies and programs, for to that extent they have compromised their standing as centers for independent criticism and surveillance of those policies and programs. The citizen has never had greater need of the protection afforded by the university than in the present epoch of centralizaton of power in the national state. But our great universities are engaged in abrogating their commitments.

125

This is a melancholy state of affairs. It has become virtually impossible for a university to turn down a federal grant, regardless of how small it is. Even the Catholic universities— once bastions of private control—have begun to rid themselves of ecclesiastical authority in order to obtain more federal aid.

The earliest, and in many ways the most influential, piece of federal aid to higher education was the Morrill Land Grant Act of 1862. Named after Justin Smith Morrill, a Vermont senator, the Morrill Act followed the lead of the Northwest Ordinance by allocating 30,000 acres of federal land to each state for each of its representatives in Congress, to establish colleges of technology and agriculture. Today there are 68 land-grant colleges and universities in all the states and Puerto Rico, making up approximately 25 percent of the college population, 20 percent of all baccalaureate degrees, 24 percent of all masters' degrees, and 40 percent of all doctorates. While the federal government presently gives only just under $20 million to these institutions today, their fundamental scope and purpose continue to be influenced by the original federal plan. It should be noted that the 68 land-grant colleges include in their number some of the most important universities in the country—Cornell, MIT, Minnesota, Wisconsin, Illinois, California. They have given the federal government a unique role both in American science and in agriculture; and since they have always been dominated by federal thinking, they have never experienced that sense of autonomy which Mr. Piel correctly attributes to the more traditional university.

The Servicemen's Readjustment Act of 1944, the so-called GI Bill of Rights, profoundly affected our nations' colleges and universities by financing the education of millions of veterans, and transforming many universities into mass institutions with huge student populations. "Since the first GI Bill," James D. Koerner has written, "our institutions of higher education have never been the same." But in many ways the influence of the GI Bill was insignificant compared with the billions of fed-

126

eral dollars spent since World War II to subsidize scientific research. The federal government served, in William Stevens' words, "as midwife to a new model of the elite university, one that became the standard of aspiration for most of the other institutions: the 'research university,' dominated by its graduate schools, sometimes neglecting undergraduate education." Many critics of the federal government's aid to scientific research, Clark Kerr among them, have blamed it for much of the trouble that has taken place on our campuses in recent years.

The development of that unique American institution, the two-year community college, specializing in commercial and technical subjects, may also be attributed to the activity of the federal government. These schools have developed rapidly over the past twenty years, and large sums of money from the Higher Education Facilities Act of 1963 have greatly spurred on their development. In 1965 alone—in large part as a result of federal stimulus—fifty new two-year colleges opened their doors to students. These schools have by the federal government, been strongly influenced in the direction of technological subjects, and they promise to play a formidable role in the future of American higher education.

A further list of federal accomplishments would be superfluous, especially since the growth of the federal role in higher education is beyond dispute. Our most pressing problem is the future direction of that role in the wake of the torrent of education legislation passed by Congress during the 1960s. It is therefore important to examine the most significant piece of federal higher education legislation to emerge from the sixties, the Higher Education Act of 1965. Much has been written about the HEA, but little in the way of serious criticism. Like all Great Society social legislation, it has been the beneficiary of a well-managed public-relations campaign which has successfully smothered criticism under a blanket of generalities. While it is still too early to get anything even vaguely resembling an overview of the HEA, we can make a few very specific judgments about its various provisions.

To begin with, the HEA calls upon our universities to join the battle against poverty and slums in our cities. Well over $10 million is being spent under Title I in order to stimulate universities into developing community-service programs. Title II spends almost $5 million to educate librarians and improve university library facilities. Title III is devoted to the one in every four of our nation's two- and four-year colleges and universities which fails to meet regional accreditation standards. In recent years millions upon millions of dollars have been spent in an effort to improve the facilities and faculties of these unaccredited institutions, many of which really deserve to go out of business. Over $60 million is spent under Title IV in order to aid needy students in completing their studies. Title V was meant to end the teacher shortage by providing close to $200 million worth of teaching fellowships and sponsoring the much debated Teacher Corps (formerly known as the National Teacher Corps, before the "national" appellation became too hot for the timid Office of Education to handle). Finally, Title VI devotes over $50 million to the proliferation of the so-called teaching machines, which may one day succeed in the complete dehumanization of the American school.

In short, the HEA has programs which influence virtually every aspect of higher education. If one adds to the HEA the influence of other free-spending federal agencies, such as the Office of Science and Technology, and the CIA, as well as such independent agencies as the Atomic Energy Commission, the Appalachian Regional Commission, the National Endowment on the Arts and the Humanities, one begins to comprehend the magnitude of the federal presence in American higher education. From the Defense Department to the National Science Foundation, it is clear that virtually every aspect of the federal government has managed to have some influence over our nation's institutions of higher learning.

Saddest of all, there seems to be no turning back for American higher education. Federal aid, our educators have discovered, can be addictive; and federal control, while sometimes annoying, can be lived with, as long as it is cushioned by federal money. The American taxpayer, who must foot the bill, has been forced to note, with wry stoicism, that the great wave of federal funding of American higher education in the 1960s was, in the end—like the great War on Poverty—punctuated with outbreaks of violence and unrest on campuses all over the country. In many cases the rioting students used the federal role as an excuse for their beastliness. Whether massive aid was the cause of, or simply an excuse for, campus unrest, the average American citizen is beginning to think that he has been shortchanged.

V

A similar condition may be seen at the elementary and secondary school levels, where Great Society education legislation —particularly the redoubtable Elementary and Secondary Education Act (ESEA) of 1965—has vastly increased the federal role, going far beyond the Smith-Hughes Act of 1917 and the George-Barden Act of 1944 (both of which were devoted to vocational schooling). While the Office of Education is still paying lip service to the men who run our local elementary and secondary schools around the country, it is becoming increasingly clear that these men are beginning to look to Washington rather than to their own school districts for advice and ideas. As Joseph Justman has written:

> The government cannot continue to make inroads into the professional function of the school in such vital matters as planning and evaluation without eventually undermining the school's will and capacity to make its own major decisions on what it needs and how to proceed. Already there

129

are schools which have shelved their own plans in haste to submit proposals more conformative to government stipulations, and others with frustrated officials whose high priority projects, under existing provisions, cannot qualify for federal assistance.

The huge sums of money made available through the ESEA suggest that local school officials may one day be forced to turn to the federal government for financial support with the same zeal they presently use in turning to it for ideological inspiration. Already, in the wake of *Serrano* v. *Priest*, Sidney Marland, the commissioner of education, can speak of a full financial partnership between the federal government and the local schools. It is said that the ESEA is the prototype for all future federal aid to education legislation: it combines the ideological prejudices of our educational establishment with enough hard cash to make it achieve at least some of its goals. While its language is often vague and nebulous, it has already done much to change the face of American schools. One has only to turn to the godfather of the recent educational revolution, Francis Keppel, to find the standard liberal view of the ESEA. "The ESEA," says Keppel, "seems to me the strategy for the future." "The [ESEA] *itself,*" he pontifically declares, "may be the answer." The answer to what? Why, to everything: poverty, segregation, illiteracy, the Other America. So a short exegesis of this voluminous piece of legislation seems in order.

Like most of the Great Society's education legislation the ESEA is permeated with the spirit of egalitarianism. Most students of the subject agree that Title I was the most important aspect of the ESEA, the part that helped to put federal aid to elementary and secondary schools on a firm footing. It was the big breakthrough in aid to public schools, one writer concluded. "It represents," William Stevens has noted, "the most massive expression so far of a basic principle of many kinds of federal aid: rectifying socially imposed inequality." Title I has, to date, spent $8.77 billion to improve schools in impoverished

130

urban and rural areas. Local school districts might receive as much as half the average current school expenditure per child in the state, multiplied by the number of school-age children in the district whose families make less than $2,000 a year. Although the money is distributed by the state and local agencies, these agencies can receive the federal money only if they agree to follow the federal formula. Many local school districts, upon agreeing to accept aid under Title I, have found themselves in the unfortunate educational position of devoting too much of their administrative and teaching time to the tiny portion of their school population that is financially and academically disadvantaged and retarded. In the long run, they feel, the so-called average student suffers. In many school districts, Title I funds have been so thinly spread that they have achieved nothing. To date there is no evidence to prove that Title I has achieved anything even slightly resembling $8.77 billion worth of good.

While the other sections of the ESEA provide for less money than Title I, little good can be said about them either. Title II is devoted to the improvement of school library facilities. At present we have a library allowance of almost $2.00 a year for each of the 50 million schoolchildren in America; Title II provides an additional $2.00 per child. Title III, or PACE (Projects to Advance Creativity in Education), as the Office of Education prefers to call it, will spend around $160 million on supplementary education centers and services in various communities. The PACE centers will be devoted to such subjects as physical education, remedial reading, educational television ("Sesame Street," that half-hour of preschool drivel, is a PACE creation), and psychological help for the needy. The federal role in educational research is stressed to the tune of well over $100 million in Title IV, which authorizes the establishment of national and regional educational research facilities. These research units faithfully reflect federal thinking, and have already begun further to implant federal ideas in the minds of our country's

131

educationists. Title V reflects the Office of Education's long-standing desire to provide a greater degree of coordination and centrality for American education. The proponents of the federal role have long argued that the *weakness* of state and local agencies is a major problem that can only be solved by massive federal intervention; to this end Title V spends around $20 million a year for *administrative aid.* Another proposal under Title V allows for the exchange of personnel between the Office of Education and various state educational departments "to establish a better understanding of programs and problems." If there are many school administrations in America still untainted by the Office of Education's ideological line, it is doubtful that Title V will allow them so to endure much longer. One day, very soon, the U. S. commissioner of education may be able to say, with the French minister of education, that he knows exactly what American students are studying at any given moment of the day.

Like the Higher Education Act, the ESEA has not been around long enough for us to draw many conclusions beyond those stated in our hasty exegesis, but it is already clear that it is the single most important piece of federal aid to education legislation in our history. If its numerous provisions are even half-realized, the American school will be drastically changed. Its tremendous power has already been felt in the fight for integrated schools. By threatening school districts with a possible refusal of ESEA funds for failing to comply with Title VI of the Civil Rights Act of 1964, which forbids discrimination in any federally assisted program, the Office of Education has been able to advance school integration faster than anyone previously thought possible. The ESEA promises to effect a social revolution in America. It may even hasten the common culture. But to date its educational validity must be left in doubt —and this, after all, ought to have been its main concern.

The NDEA, as previously mentioned, must be included in any discussion of the federal role in American education. The millions of dollars spent under Title III of this act have greatly influenced school programs in science, mathematics, and modern languages. Subjects previously unstudied, such as the Russian language, have become mainstays of the school curriculum, while once popular subjects, like Latin, have receded into oblivion. (A study commissioned by the Office of Education noted that during the first two decades of this century more than half of all high school students studied Latin; by 1962 only 26 percent studied Latin; today Latin is a truly dead language in America.) The potent NDEA programs have been augmented by the ESEA to create a combination of forces that will dominate American education for years to come.

VI

Educationally speaking, as Daniel P. Moynihan and Frederick Mosteller have demonstrated in their widely publicized reanalysis of James Coleman's report *Equality of Educational Opportunity,* the public has not been getting good educational value for its tax money. Coleman personified the spirit of the sixties with his great emphasis on a federal financial role. The social scientists contributing to the Moynihan-Mosteller study have sadly concluded that, despite the huge sums of money being pumped into our schools, American education has made no substantial improvements in those areas in which the federal government most wanted to see improvement. The least helpful thing you can do for American education, one contributor noted, with obvious frustration, is to spend more money on it. Education, Kenneth Boulding has lamented, may in fact be a "pathological sector of the economy in which investment brings no greater ... returns." Massive investment may do more harm than good. So why, you may ask, have the taxpayers been required to make so many sacrifices for the sake of something that may do more harm than good?

133

The answer to this question has become more obvious in recent years. The liberal myths of the 1930s managed to survive into the sixties. In a very real sense, the so-called Great Society, with its messianic approach to foreign and domestic policy, was in fact the last gasp of the New Deal.* It was believed, as an article of faith, that all we had to do to improve our society was to improve our schools, and this was best achieved by pumping more money into our schools. From the schools, it was hoped, would emerge the common culture that American liberals had dreamed of for so many years. Well, like just about everything else connected with the Johnson Administration, this massive aid to education program has not only failed, it appears to have backfired. The failure is still not so apparent as the failures of the Vietnam War and the War on Poverty, but it is apparent nevertheless. The message has not yet reached most of our educators, who continue to press for a greater federal role, proving that some myths die hard. Perhaps in ten years' time the findings of the Moynihan-Mosteller report will reach our educational establishment. But by then it may be too late. We cannot continue to view education as the Great Equalizer and expect it to fulfill its primary educational responsibilities at the same time.

*See my article, "A Memo to the Ripon Society on the Death of American Liberalism," *The Alternative* (April 1972), pp. 5, 6. The death of liberalism, I noted, has been one of the most ignored events of our time. "Not only has nobody bothered to write about it, nobody really seems to care very much. The passing of American Liberalism has evoked no mourning among its former disciples, no eloquent panegyrics, not even a doleful obituary in the *New York Times*. . . . The Liberalism that grew up in American soil . . . was a corrupted Liberalism that owed much more to our native self-righteousness than to the political philosophy advanced by the 19th-century Classical Liberals. As a people we have always viewed ourselves and our political system as being about as perfect as anything on God's Earth. Indeed, we have depicted ourselves as God's Elect. We are, in short, the embodiment of the Weberian Protestant Ethic. . . . So when Liberalism came to America, it was quickly Calvinized, and the resulting ideology had very little in common with, say, John Stuart Mill or Adam Smith. What developed in its place was an ill-considered amalgam of Goodman Brown–like Protestantism, old-fashioned imperialism . . . and a kind of watered-down socialism; and it is this intellectual hodgepodge that we Americans call Liberalism."

As federal power continues its rapid expansion, more general questions come to mind. "If, in a national society," Daniel Bell asks, "so much has to be done at the 'center,' what is left for the local community? Can we assume that such matters as policy, funding, and standards are set by the federal government, while operations are distributed throughout other levels of government?" What future role will the federal government play in American education? "If the government is going to appropriate large sums of money for education and science," Professor Bell continues, "does it have a right to set standards in the way, say, the Securities and Exchange Commission sets standards for business, or to set vocational goals by increasing student subsidies in order to encourage entry into 'socially desirable' occupations? Who is to set educational . . . policy?" This is a question that all Americans will have to consider in the years to come.

An examination of the federal role in American education as of this date seems to provide us with at least some tentative answer to Professor Bell's questions. I say tentative, because there is always the possibility that the failure of the federal aid programs presently on the books to achieve anything of educational value may help to bring about some decentralization, a renaissance of local control and individual initiative. Somehow I doubt that this will come to pass. The present trend seems to be leading us toward an even larger federal role in the years to come. The federal aid to education legislation most certainly *will* attempt to steal the initiative from the local communities; it will endeavor to regulate curriculums; and it will encourage entry into such "socially desirable" occupations as the spirit of the times considers to be socially desirable. There is a strong possibility that the essential egalitarianism of most of the federal legislation will bring about a dilution of academic standards. Perhaps the common culture will arrive at long last?

It seems highly unlikely, but it is possible that a significant portion of our educational establishment could follow the lead of Clark Kerr and become disillusioned with the entire concept of a federal role in our schools. This is unlikely because the educational establishment seems to have almost total faith in the capacity of the government to do good. "When the state undertakes to achieve a goal and fails," George Stigler has remarked, "we cannot bring ourselves to abandon the goal.... We demand . . . increased efforts of the state tacitly assuming that where there is a will, there is a governmental way." Which is to say, regardless of how many times our federal aid to education programs fail to accomplish those ends that they set out to accomplish in the first place, there will always be more cash with which to start the ball rolling all over again. As P. T. Barnum used to say, "There's a sucker born every minute."

VII

It may prove instructive, in conclusion, to turn away from our educationists, and to muse upon the wisdom of one of our century's most astute cultural critics, the late T. S. Eliot. Eliot, along with his friend Bernard Iddings Bell, had become very disenchanted about the growing role of the state in education, which he viewed as a modern form of Jacobinism. Where the Deweyites saw the common culture, Eliot perceived a cultural breakdown: where the educationists saw greater equality, Eliot saw the disintegration of true culture. "There is a danger," he explained, "that education—which [has come under] the influence of politics—will take upon itself the reformation and direction of culture, instead of keeping its place as one of the activities through which culture realizes itself. Culture cannot altogether be brought to consciousness; and the culture of which we are wholly conscious is never the whole of culture; the effective culture is that which is directing the activities of those who are manipulating that which they call culture."

And yet this is exactly what is happening in America: the

136

Office of Education, supplied with vast amounts of federal money, has undertaken to reform our culture in the name of education. Perhaps Eliot's version of the future was more pessimistic than we would have it; but who can deny, in the wake of recent developments, the soundness of his concluding prophecy. "There is no doubt," he declared, "that in our headlong rush to educate everybody, we are lowering the standards, and more and more abandoning the study of those subjects which are the essentials of our culture . . .; destroying our ancient edifices to make ready the ground upon which the barbarian nomads of the future will encamp in their mechanized caravans."

A STATISTICAL PRIMER ON

PUBLIC ELEMENTARY AND SECONDARY EDUCATION IN THE UNITED STATES

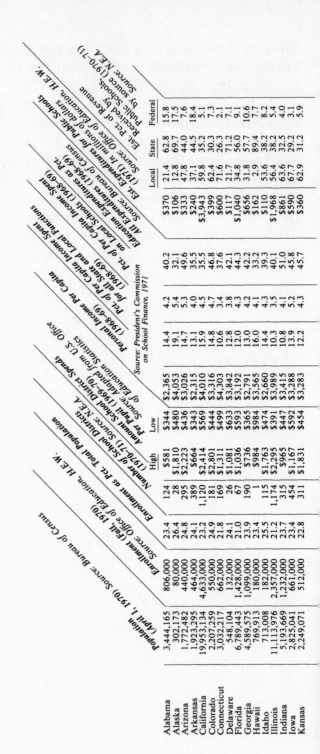

State	Population (April 1, 1970) Source: Bureau of Census	Enrollment (fall, 1970) Source: Office of Education, H.E.W.	Enrollment as Pct. Total Population	Number of School Districts (1970-71) Source: N.E.A.	Amount School District Spends per Pupil (1969-70) High	Amount School District Spends per Pupil (1969-70) Low	Personal Income Per Capita (1968-69)	Pct. of per Capita Income Spent for all State and Local Functions (1968-69)	Pct. of per Capita Income Spent on Local Schools (1968-69)	All Expenditures (1968-69)	Education Expenditures (1968-69)	Local	State	Federal
Alabama	3,444,165	806,000	23.4	124	$581	$344	$2,365	14.4	4.2	40.2	$370	21.4	62.8	15.8
Alaska	302,173	80,000	26.4	28	$1,810	$480	$4,053	19.1	5.4	32.1	$106	12.8	69.7	17.5
Arizona	1,772,482	440,000	24.8	295	$2,223	$436	$3,026	14.7	5.3	49.6	$333	47.8	44.0	7.6
Arkansas	1,923,295	464,000	24.1	389	$664	$343	$2,315	13.1	4.0	35.5	$240	37.1	44.5	18.4
California	19,953,134	4,633,000	23.2	1,120	$2,414	$569	$4,010	15.9	4.5	35.5	$3,943	59.8	35.2	5.1
Colorado	2,207,259	550,000	24.9	181	$2,801	$444	$3,316	14.8	4.7	46.8	$399	62.4	30.3	7.3
Connecticut	3,032,217	662,000	21.8	169	$1,311	$499	$4,303	10.6	3.4	37.6	$600	71.6	26.3	2.1
Delaware	548,104	132,000	24.1	26	$1,081	$633	$3,842	12.8	3.8	42.1	$117	21.7	71.2	7.1
Florida	6,789,443	1,428,000	21.0	67	$1,036	$593	$3,192	12.0	4.3	44.3	$1,040	34.8	56.0	9.1
Georgia	4,589,575	1,099,000	23.9	190	$736	$365	$2,791	13.0	4.2	42.2	$656	31.8	57.7	10.6
Hawaii	769,913	180,000	23.4	1	$984	$984	$3,565	16.0	4.1	33.2	$162	2.9	89.4	7.7
Idaho	713,008	182,000	25.5	115	$1,763	$474	$2,660	16.4	4.3	39.3	$110	53.6	38.2	8.2
Illinois	11,113,976	2,357,000	21.2	1,174	$2,295	$391	$3,989	10.3	3.5	40.1	$1,968	56.4	38.2	5.4
Indiana	5,193,669	1,232,000	23.7	315	$965	$447	$3,415	10.8	4.1	51.0	$861	63.6	32.5	4.0
Iowa	2,825,041	661,000	23.4	454	$1,167	$592	$3,288	13.9	5.2	45.8	$590	67.7	29.2	3.1
Kansas	2,249,071	512,000	22.8	311	$1,831	$454	$3,283	12.2	4.3	45.7	$360	62.9	31.2	5.9

Amount School District Spends per Pupil (1969-70) Source: Education Statistics adapted from U.S. Office of Education

Est. Expenditures (1971) in millions of dollars Source: Bureau of Census

Source: President's Commission on School Finance, 1971

Est. Pct. of Revenue Received by Public Schools by Source (1970-71) Source: N.E.A.

Kentucky	3,219,311	717,000	22.3	192	$885	$358	$2,630	13.2	4.0	40.1	$404	31.6	55.0	13.5
Louisiana	3,643,180	843,000	23.1	66	$892	$499	$2,644	15.6	4.6	37.5	$621	28.8	60.0	11.2
Maine	993,663	245,000	24.7	288	$1,555	$229	$2,830	13.7	4.0	39.7	$175	60.1	31.9	7.9
Maryland	3,922,399	916,000	23.4	24	$1,037	$635	$3,780	12.3	4.3	41.7	$808	58.9	35.3	5.8
Massachusetts	5,689,170	1,168,000	20.5	416	$1,281	$515	$3,888	13.8	3.3	29.8	$938	72.3	21.7	6.1
Michigan	8,875,083	2,181,000	24.6	630	$1,364	$491	$3,715	13.4	4.5	47.5	$1,879	50.9	45.5	3.7
Minnesota	3,805,069	921,000	24.2	500	$903	$370	$3,346	14.6	5.3	45.0	$896	51.9	43.4	4.6
Mississippi	2,216,912	535,000	24.1	150	$825	$283	$2,074	15.4	4.8	39.7	$263	25.2	52.4	22.4
Missouri	4,677,399	1,039,000	22.2	621	$1,699	$213	$3,264	11.7	4.0	42.7	$686	59.4	32.2	8.4
Montana	694,409	177,000	25.4	744	$1,716	$539	$2,906	14.5	5.0	40.9	$142	68.0	24.0	8.0
Nebraska	1,483,791	329,000	22.2	1,700	$1,175	$623	$3,200	13.1	4.5	45.9	$214	75.8	17.6	6.6
Nevada	488,738	127,000	26.0	17	$1,679	$746	$3,971	15.0	4.1	33.2	$95	56.3	36.8	6.9
New Hampshire	737,681	159,000	21.6	168	$1,191	$311	$3,272	11.1	3.2	41.4	$106	86.2	9.6	4.3
New Jersey	7,168,164	1,482,000	20.7	599	$1,485	$400	$3,968	10.4	3.8	40.0	$1,530	69.2	25.9	4.9
New Mexico	1,016,000	282,000	27.8	89	$1,183	$477	$2,666	18.4	6.4	48.5	$209	20.0	63.4	16.6
New York	18,190,740	3,477,000	19.1	760	$1,889	$669	$4,141	16.2	4.6	33.9	$4,336	47.7	47.9	4.3
North Carolina	5,082,059	1,192,000	23.5	152	$733	$467	$2,658	11.2	3.9	46.8	$713	18.8	66.2	15.0
North Dakota	617,761	147,000	23.8	411	$1,623	$686	$2,657	18.3	5.2	41.9	$98	66.2	25.8	8.0
Ohio	10,652,017	2,425,000	22.8	631	$1,685	$413	$3,480	10.5	3.8	42.2	$1,750	66.5	28.3	4.7
Oklahoma	2,559,253	627,000	24.5	665	$2,566	$342	$2,833	14.9	4.1	39.8	$385	46.7	43.5	9.8
Oregon	2,091,385	479,000	22.9	350	$1,439	$399	$3,325	15.3	5.3	47.1	$411	74.5	19.6	5.9
Pennsylvania	11,793,909	2,358,000	20.0	597	$1,401	$484	$3,394	11.2	4.0	41.6	$2,089	47.8	46.2	6.0
Rhode Island	949,723	188,000	19.8	40	$1,206	$531	$3,611	12.5	3.2	35.4	$164	57.8	36.5	5.7
South Carolina	2,590,516	638,000	24.6	93	$610	$397	$2,391	12.1	4.4	47.0	$392	25.4	61.7	13.0
South Dakota	666,257	166,000	24.9	286	$1,741	$350	$2,820	16.0	5.6	46.5	$113	73.9	15.1	10.9
Tennessee	3,924,164	900,000	22.9	147	$766	$315	$2,584	12.0	3.8	40.4	$510	40.3	47.1	12.6
Texas	11,196,730	2,840,000	25.4	1,187	$5,334	$264	$3,019	11.0	4.0	45.9	$1,578	40.7	49.3	10.0
Utah	1,059,273	304,000	28.7	40	$1,515	$533	$2,793	15.6	5.7	53.2	$185	39.8	54.7	5.5
Vermont	444,732	103,000	23.2	277	$1,517	$357	$3,053	15.0	3.9	39.4	$108	63.5	33.9	2.5
Virginia	4,648,494	1,078,000	23.2	134	$1,126	$441	$3,074	10.8	3.9	44.6	$810	54.2	35.2	10.6
Washington	3,409,169	818,000	24.0	321	$3,406	$434	$3,674	13.4	4.5	45.5	$665	37.7	56.6	5.7
West Virginia	1,744,237	399,000	22.9	55	$722	$502	$2,433	14.4	4.7	42.0	$238	38.9	48.8	12.3
Wisconsin	4,417,933	993,000	22.5	455	$1,432	$344	$3,374	15.1	4.4	44.7	$872	67.7	29.3	3.1
Wyoming	332,416	86,000	25.9	131		$618	$3,100	19.1	6.1	35.4	$76	51.6	25.8	22.6
U.S.	202,428,262	45,904,000	22.7	17,895	$14,554		$3,425	13.2	4.2	40.5	$44,424	52.0	44.1	6.9

7

The American Challenge

Today in America . . . a new revolution is rising.

JEAN-FRANCOIS REVEL

Since the end of World War II, American civilization, in all its varied manifestations, has profoundly influenced the rest of the world. The pervasive impact of our culture on other cultures in the postwar world is a phenomenon without parallel in modern history, creating what the late Henry Luce called "the American century." From the omnipresent Coca-Cola bottle to Hershey bars, comic strips, popular music, literature, and motion pictures, the American image, or, at very least, a somewhat distorted version of that image, has succeeded in influencing friend and foe alike. This altered version of the American image has, on occasion, come back to haunt us—like our reflection in a sideshow mirror—reminding us more of our weaknesses than of our strengths.

Paradoxically, our popularity has never managed to equal our influence. Our critics have generally outnumbered our friends, and our friends have never been as influential as our critics. The pro-American euphoria that followed our victory over fascism in World War II was short-lived, and was succeeded, especially among the intellectuals of Western Europe, by a wave of expertly contrived anti-Americanism. The American people were depicted as simpleminded vulgarians, lacking in sophistication and social grace; our institutions were portrayed as being corrupt and archaic; and our political leaders and their policies were subjected to vilification in left-wing newspapers throughout the world. Nevertheless, the progress of American influence continued unabated, transcending all the anti-American vituperation and swaying even the most ardent enemies of the American cause.

In the wake of World War II there was much talk in Europe about revolution. But the revolution never came. The so-called revolutionaries—the very same people who spearheaded the anti-American movement—had, in truth, ceased to be revolutionary. The large Communist parties of Italy and France talked about democratic alternatives to revolutions, and the European left, in general, struck other leftists as being, at best, bourgeois, at worst, counterrevolutionary.[1] It was at this point that many leftists began to contemplate the American situation in a new light. Jean-Jacques Servan-Schreiber, the influential publisher of the French newsweekly *L'Express,* hinted that America was the only genuine revolutionary force in the world. In his bestselling book, *The American Challenge,* he warned Europeans that America would soon be a more powerful European force than Europe itself. He was speaking specifically of American technology and industry in Europe, but he was also pointing a finger at the spirit that had helped make America as influential a force as it had already, at that time, become. Americans were *not,* he argued, the stupid stereotypes that Europeans had become accustomed to reading about in various left-wing journals. Rather, they were an intelligent, a well-educated, and an industrious people. Instead of making fun of America and Americans, Europe ought to pattern itself after them. In the field of education, Servan-Schreiber was particu-

1. In May of 1968, when students at the Nanterre campus of the Sorbonne began a revolution that was to shake France, and then the rest of Europe, the French Communist Party, along with its powerful trade union, the CGT, refused to join them, and even went so far as to attack them and to support the Gaullist establishment in its moves to put the revolution down.

larly taken with the egalitarian and instrumental nature of American education, which he declared to be much better than the elitist French system.

But M. Servan-Schreiber was not alone in his enthusiasm for "revolutionary" America. His *L'Express* colleague Jean-Francois Revel—who was more interested in revolution than technology—suggested that left-wing European intellectuals were backing the wrong revolutionary horse.[2] America, and *not* the Soviet Union, would lead the *real* revolution of our century. "Today in America," he explained,

> a new revolution is rising. It is *the* revolution of our time. It is the only revolution that involves radical, moral, and practical opposition to the spirit of nationalism. It is the only revolution that, to that opposition, joins culture, economic and technological power, and a total affirmation of liberty for all in place of archaic prohibitions. It therefore offers the only possible escape for mankind today: the acceptance of technological civilization as a means and not an end, and . . . the development of the ability to reshape that civilization without annihilating it.[3]

The United States, for Revel, was the prototype nation for the revolution of our time because of its wealth, its rate of growth, its technology, its culture, its orientation toward the future rather than the past, its egalitarianism, its modern lifestyle, and its numerous subcultures. "There are five revolutions that must take place either simultaneously or not at all," he cautioned: "[a] political revolution; a social revolution; a technological and scientific revolution; a revolution in culture, values, and standards; and a revolution in international and interracial relations." The United States, he announced, is the only country where these various revolutions are all presently tak-

2. Peter P. Witonski, "The Trendy Revolution," *National Review,* December 3, 1971, pp. 1361–62.
3. Jean-Francois Revel, *Without Marx or Jesus: The New American Revolution Has Begun* (Garden City, N. Y.: Doubleday & Co., 1971), p. 242.

ing place, constituting a single revolution, the revolution of our time.[4]

The new American revolution that Revel observed has nothing in common with the classic eighteenth- and nineteenth-century models of what a revolution ought to be. Rather, it is a revolution in progress, *our* revolution, *the* revolution of the twentieth century, and thus "the only possible escape for mankind." The American dikes, he declared, have broken, and soon the waters of the American revolution will flood the world. For Europeans, especially for M. Revel's friends on the European left, this was the essence of the challenge posed by the United States. They could hold fast to their anti-Americanism, and build their own fortifications against the deluge; or they could recognize the revolutionary implications of the new American left, and be carried off on the wave of the future.[5]

Revel, like so many contemporary ideologists, seems unable to come to grips with the dynamics of western civilization. His ideal society is a society that is alien to everything western civilization stands for. Neither Marx nor Jesus will be accepted by his wave of the future. Indeed, he thinks he has discovered in the United States a society that has rejected both Marx and Jesus. All of which seems to suggest that Revel's understanding of America is blurred, perhaps by reason of the fact that he traveled in bad company during his several visits to this country. There are elements in American society that have indeed rejected both Marx and Jesus, or rejected Jesus and accepted Marx, but they in no way represent the aspirations of the

4. *Ibid.,* pp. 183–184.
5. Europeans, Revel surmised, would probably not share his enthusiasm for the new American revolution. "The most humiliating kind of defeat," he wrote, "is cultural defeat. . . . It entails not only acknowledgment of one's own weakness, but also the humiliation of having to save oneself by taking lessons from the conqueror—whom one must simultaneously hate and imitate. It was for that reason that *The American Challenge* was virtuously denounced and, at the same time, avidly read." *Ibid.,* pp. 139 ff.

American people, for whom Marx means nothing and Jesus at least a good man. But this takes nothing away from Revel's basic thesis, since he is not interested in the views of the American majority. It is the tiny leftist minority that inspires Revel, and distorts his understanding of America. Out of this minority, he hopes, will come a revolutionary matrix that can be applied to Europe.

What Revel found on his trips to America was a society that most Americans would consider to be a Hobbesian nightmare land, representing the darker side of American life. Revel's America was a place that was barbarized to the point where the only true heroes were nature's villains—New Left intellectuals, Weathermen, urban rioters, campus nihilists, jailhouse authors. Juxtaposed against them, he argued, was a dying conservatism, which must eventually succumb to the *Zeitgeist.*

Needless to say, Revel's findings initiated a series of controversies on both sides of the Atlantic. Mary McCarthy, representing the American left that Revel admired so much, penned an afterword to the American edition of *Without Marx or Jesus,* claiming that it was one big practical joke. She, like so many of Revel's European critics, failed to recognize that Revel was consciously magnifying the left-wing role in American society in order to take potshots at what he considered to be the sterile and counterrevolutionary European left. What Revel, and just about everybody else, failed to recognize was that those aspects of American life which he considered to be revolutionary had already begun to make their impact felt throughout Europe. In a certain sense the American left was having a greater impact on Europe than on America. The revolutionary soil was more fertile in nations like France, Germany, Italy, and Britain, where the left had traditionally been more influential than in America. To the extent that Revel was himself a product of the Old Left, he failed to comprehend the force of the New Left. He himself was simply out of touch.

By the early sixties the new American left had already begun

144

to catch the attention of European students. They were reading American books, listening to American music, wearing American-style clothing, even sharing American social and political causes. American issues that were not really related to Europe had begun to interest them. The black revolution, the drug culture, the anti-Vietnam movement all affected European students. The heroes of the American left, such as Herbert Marcuse, Eldridge Cleaver, and Timothy Leary, became European heroes, often surpassing home-grown products in popularity. America, as one conservative observer noted, was not simply exporting Coca-Cola and rock music; it was also sending over its new ideologies and causes, and these were catching on as rapidly as Coca-Cola had in the years after World War II.

II

Historically, Europeans have viewed the American experiment in educational egalitarianism with great skepticism. Before World War II it was fashionable for well-educated Europeans to look down their noses on American universities, as places where quantity was prized more highly than quality, where football and fraternities held sway over the grand old classical education. Equality of educational opportunity may be, it was argued, a noble ideal, but there is no way of achieving it without transforming institutions of learning into places of uniformity and mediocrity. Europe had nothing to learn from American educational theories. In truth, our entire educational system was viewed as an enormous intellectual joke.

But World War II changed all that. Europe's great centers of learning had been seriously hurt, and in some cases totally destroyed, by the war. A gigantic vacuum existed, and, as has been noted, American educationalists all abhor vacuums. In the years following the war crusading American educationalists rushed to the aid of European education with vast sums of

145

money, advice, and, in the case of Germany, near total control.[6] Private foundations and federal agencies encouraged European educators to Americanize their institutions—or, as it was usually put, to *modernize* them. Fulbright professors and scholars, American textbooks and teaching methods flooded into Europe, becoming a major force throughout the Continent. Even such ancient universities as Oxford and Cambridge, which had not been seriously hurt by the war, felt the force of Americanization. By the 1960s, most of the great schools and universities of Europe had been at least partially Americanized.

Theories and approaches to learning that had once been maligned were gradually accepted, paving the way for greater American influence in other sectors of European social and intellectual life; and while the thrust of American educational innovation had its detractors, it had many more advocates in positions of power and influence. Some of the champions of Americanization followed the lead of M. Servan-Schreiber in holding up the technological instrumentalism of American education. European students, Servan-Schreiber and his followers argued, were wasting their time studying classical literature and French poetry, while American students were mastering such useful subjects as business administration. Other Americanizers followed the lead of M. Revel in glorifying the more sinister aspects of American education. While students at the Sorbonne must study such traditional subjects as mathematics and history, they noted, American students may avail themselves of courses in filmmaking, acting, and folk music.

6. After the war Dr. James B. Conant, who was to play such a large role in altering the course of American education, played an equally significant role in the Americanization of German education, particularly at the university level. In his essay, written in German, *Probleme der Universitäten in Deutschland und in den USA* (Tubingen, 1965), he reviews his success, and makes further suggestions. Also of importance in tracing the impact of Americanization on Germany's universities is Rudolf L. Mössbauer's *Strukturprobleme der deutschen Universität* (Bremen, 1965).

European education would never be the same again. In our messianic urge to make the world safe for democracy, we had only succeeded in ruining some of the greatest institutions of learning in the world, institutions from which much that was once excellent in American education had originally been stimulated.[7] Today much that is wrong with European education, especially at the university level, may be placed at the door of the Americanizers, *especially* the European advocates of Americanization.

III

The seriousness of the American challenge to European education was not fully perceived until the rise of the New Left. The New Left was indeed *new,* and in a very real sense its origins could be traced to America. Its revolutionary ideology was the very same ideology that had been rejected as "ultraleftist" by the various European Communist parties during the 1930s. Indeed, its leading intellectual spokesman, Professor Herbert Marcuse, had long been considered an ideological renegade by orthodox Marxists. Tolerance of dissent, Marcuse argued in his essay *Repressive Tolerance,* is a manifestation of bourgeois democracy; it is the method by which the establishment stays in power. "Within a repressive society," he argued, "even progressive movements threaten to turn into their opposite to the degree to which they accept the rules of the game. To take a most conventional case: the exercise of political

7. The so-called Free University of Berlin provides a classic example of our good intentions backfiring on us. Founded after the war with vast sums of money from the American government and the Ford Foundation, the Free University was expected to develop into the model Americanized European university. It was to be a place where the spirit of freedom and democracy was championed and spread to other German universities. In fact, it has become the most undemocratic university in Germany, and the fountainhead of much of the student unrest that has plagued Germany in recent years. It has also become a bastion of anti-Americanism.

rights (such as voting, letterwriting to the press, to senators, etc., protest demonstrations with *a priori* renunciation of counterviolence) in a society of total administration serves to strengthen the administration by testifying to the existence of democratic liberties . . . in such case, freedom (of opinion, of assembly, of speech) becomes an instrument for absolving servitude."

For the New Left, the enemy was freedom, or, as Marcuse typically put it, "the democratic educational dictatorship of free men." Recognizing the unpopularity of his views, Marcuse declared that "liberation would mean subversion against the will and against the great majority of the people." In many ways this attitude is very much akin to fascism. "The people be damned," Marcuse seemed to be saying. Only he preferred to express such views in his own pedestrian prose style. The New Left revolution will have arrived, he wrote, "where the people cannot reject the system of domination without rejecting themselves, their own instinctual needs and values." But bourgeois democracy will not let this happen. "The semidemocratic process," he wrote,

> works of necessity against radical change because it produces and sustains a popular majority whose opinion is generated by the dominant interests of the *status quo*. As long as this condition prevails, it makes sense to say that *the general will is always wrong* . . . capitalist mass-democracy is perhaps to a higher degree self-perpetuating than any other form of government or society; and the more so the more it rests, not on terror and scarcity, but on efficiency and wealth, and on the *majority will* of the underlying and administered population. [Italics added]

It is nasty drivel like this, as Warden John Sparrow of All Souls described it, that fueled the engines of the new student left. The Marcusean ideology, of course, could have started only in a rich country like America, where Orthodox communism was, in Daniel Cohn-Bendit's phrase, "obsolete," devoid of any real chance of succeeding. Only in America, where students were rich (by European standards), badly educated, and guilty

148

about their country's affluence, could the Orwellian cry "Toleration is Oppression" take hold. But as European students became more Americanized, more affluent, and less well educated, the appeal of the Marcusean New Left began to become more obvious to them also. And of course as Europe, like America, became more affluent and more democratic, the traditional idea of revolution became more obsolete. After all, what was the point of getting rid of a good thing.

The significance of Herbert Marcuse for New Leftists like Eldridge Cleaver, Regis Debray, Rudi Dutschke, and Cohn-Bendit was that he articulated—admittedly in that lugubriously dull way of his—the frustration of the revolutionary in the society that wants nothing to do with revolutionary nostrums. America had helped to bring prosperity to Europe, and so America had made Europeans counterrevolutionists. But there was another side to the coin. The authorities, both in America and in Europe, seemed not to know how to stop the New Left's minirevolution, despite the fact that nobody wanted to see a revolution. During the Paris uprising in May 1969, a famous wall poster read, "Soyez realistes: demandez l'impossible." The revolution was impossible, but nobody seemed to know how to cope with it, and so it continued apace, even where it was not wanted.

IV

Before 1968 most European educators looked upon the violent events then taking place on American campuses with a sense of superiority. Many of them had not yet recognized the extent to which their own institutions and student populations had been Americanized. For many of them, America remained the New World, barbarously provincial, and totally uninteresting. Those who bothered to think about events in America at all, blamed campus unrest on the war in Vietnam and on black militancy, noting that these were American problems, twin

149

manifestations of America's immaturity. "It can't happen here," they argued, with some satisfaction.

But, of course, campus unrest did come to Europe, and it was obvious that the campus unrest of the late sixties was very different from the kind of campus unrest that had taken place in the twenties and thirties. Since a large portion of the youth of Europe had at least been partially Americanized by the sixties, it followed that the revolutionaries among them would also be at least partially Americanized. The fact that they were militantly anti-American was of little importance. After all, the most vicious anti-Americanism of all had come from America in the first place, where the New Left and its radical-chic patrons were making a cult out of their own hatred of America and American values. It could be argued that every anti-American slogan used by the European left was first used by the American New Left.[8]

Indeed, American anti-Americanism was to play a central role both in developing an ideology for the European student rebels and in converting them to the American model of student protest and rebellion. It is clear that the European student left, unlike its leftist elders, wanted very much to be swept along by the new revolution that Jean-Francois Revel and others had discovered in America. But that is not all the student left wanted. It wanted very much to expand upon America's New Leftism, which many student leftists rightly saw as a massive series of mindless eruptions without any central set of ideological goals. The European leftists had philosophized, rather in the tradition of M. Revel, about the supposed evils and virtues of America; American leftists merely felt guilty.[9] Revo-

8. For an excellent analysis of American anti-Americanism, see Arnold Beichman's *Nine Lies about America* (Freeport, N. Y.: Library Press, 1972).
9. For a typical compendium of New Leftist guilt, see Robert Coles' and Daniel Berrigan's running dialogue, *The Geography of Faith* (Boston: Beacon Press, 1971). At one point Berrigan asks psychiatrist Coles, "Why are there no psychiatrists in prison today?" Coles responds to this insipid (*pace* Thoreau) question with an outpouring of shame and guilt.

lutions, insisted Europeans like Cohn-Bendit, should be made
of sterner stuff.

V

One should not be too hard on European educators for failing
to notice the American challenge to their universities before it
was too late. After all, most American educators had been tardy
in recognizing the true danger of the student left. The real
question is not *why* they were not better prepared to counter
the student left, but, rather, *how* their seemingly peaceful campuses became "radicalized" at all. To answer this question we
will consider a university that had experienced no major student problems in the fifties and early sixties, and that had no
real reason for emulating the American situation, but that became radicalized, or at least partially radicalized, despite all
this.

Oxford University is England's senior university, one of the
most ancient and traditional universities in the world.[10] Its academic standards are among the highest in Europe, and its students represent the very best Britain has to offer. Living
conditions, on the whole, are excellent. Thanks to the old medieval college system, Oxford has managed to avoid the evils of
Clark Kerr's Multiversity. It is a big university, but not big to
the extent of being dehumanized. The teacher-student ratio is
excellent and, by and large, students have no problems (again
thanks to the college system) in meeting even the most famous
professors and dons. The ancient tutorial system provides
added personalization in that it requires undergraduate students to meet once a week with an assigned tutor who guides

10. I have chosen Oxford University, not only because it seemed the place least
likely to experience student unrest, but also because it is the European university I know best. As a graduate student there during the last four years of the
sixties, I had ample opportunity to observe the growth of an Americanized
student left in its ancient colleges.

his charges through their academic chores, and advises them on their personal and academic problems. Finally, along with Cambridge, it is a place where ancient custom and tradition have managed to survive, despite the modernizing pressures of the twentieth century. In short, it is not the sort of place where one would expect to find student rebels.

In fact, there were no *real* student rebels when I arrived there for the first time in 1965. To be sure, there were campus leftists, but they were rather polite, and tended to associate themselves mainly with the Labour Party and democratic socialism. There was no real reason for rebelling. Oxford seemed to be about as perfect as a university could be. Nevertheless, as early as 1965, the student of campus politics could begin to detect certain subtle changes in student opinion. They were of two kinds. The most serious revolutionaries had begun to explore the literature of the New Left, particularly such American sources as Herbert Marcuse and C. Wright Mills. The least serious revolutionaries were those who were looking for kicks. Both groups looked longingly to America, where buildings were being burned and deans were being defenestrated. In a phrase, they felt out of it, and they wanted in. It must be fun, one would hear leftist students say, to seize buildings and fight cops. The problem was that they had no following.

There were numerous attempts to turn Oxford students on to revolution, all of them unsuccessful. One possible explanation for this failure—aside from the fact that conditions were pretty good at Oxford—was that most of the militant students were not British. The leading Oxford leftist in the midsixties was a thick-headed and wealthy Pakistani named Tarik Ali, and he was generally written off by everybody, save possibly the headline-hungry British press, as a bloody bore. Although Ali's followers included several British students, they were not among the most articulate or clever at the university. Indeed, if the student left at Oxford had any motivating force, it came mainly from American troublemakers fresh from the student wars on

152

their American campuses. Before 1968 the most significant New Leftist group on campus was an organization calling itself the Stop-It Committee, made up almost entirely of Americans whose sympathies lay with the Viet Cong. But since Britain was in no way involved in the Vietnam War, Stop-It remained a rather marginal organization.

Of course, as students of the New Left know, the Vietnam War was not so much the cause as the excuse for much of the campus unrest in America. The roots of student rebellion run far deeper. A combination of youthful conformity and exuberance is probably the main motivating factor. In America before leftism was apotheosized in pop music and in the press, most students had no interest in demonstrating for left-wing causes; but when it became *in* to be a leftist, a surprisingly large number of students conformed to what they thought was the stylish thing to do. During the midsixties, New Leftism was not *in* at Oxford, and so the campus left never amounted to anything. But as large numbers of Oxford students surveyed the left-wing scene in America and other countries, it is clear that they began to feel out of the swim of things, and there is nothing a young student hates more than being an outsider.

In the spring of 1968, shortly before the Paris uprising, I was sitting in the Oxford Union talking with several of the leading campus leftists. They were a very embittered lot. This was at the time when Columbia University and the University of Berlin were undergoing serious campus rebellions. "Why," one of the leftists asked me, "can't we have a strike or something at Oxford?" It was a good question. Other British universities, especially the London School of Economics and the notoriously left-wing University of Essex, had had some real campus violence. Oxford had traditionally been the prime mover in British politics. Was Oxford to be the only peaceful university in Britain? This last question particularly intrigued the press and the BBC, which had made every student in Britain aware of the events taking place in America and Germany by publicizing

153

them out of proportion. "A student rebellion at Essex," a British journalist informed me at the time, "is simply not front-page material. But a student rebellion at Oxford would really sell papers."

Everybody seemed to be waiting for Oxford to rebel. Every incident taking place on American campuses was publicized to the nth degree. It was impossible not to be aware of the leaders of campus rebellions even at obscure American colleges. A new kind of celebrity was being born. He was a long-haired, pot-smoking, hip campus revolutionary, with a peace button on his dirty undershirt and an electric bullhorn in his hand. For the campus leftists at Oxford the troubles in America, coupled with the Sorbonne uprising, were the giddy limit. Something had to be done. And so on the spring Bank Holiday in 1968, ten students staged a demonstration in front of Bodleian Library. Since it was a Bank Holiday, which meant that literally every shop in Oxford was closed down, there was nobody there to witness the demonstration. Nobody, that is, except the representatives of the British press.

The following day the demonstration, the actual cause of which nobody ever really got around to fully explaining, was headlined on the front pages of every newspaper in Britain. The ten demonstrators were interviewed by the BBC and the ITV, and overnight ten stars were born, along with a genuine New Left at Oxford. "Oxford University," they jointly declared, "is a repressive and fascistic institution." Within the week, the ten became a hundred, and the authorities suddenly discovered that they had a potential problem on their hands.

The British press, particularly the BBC, was not satisfied. There was something artificial about the Bank Holiday demonstration. The Oxford student rebels lacked the gusto of American and Continental student leftists. And so, in the wake of the Paris uprising, an enterprising executive at the BBC decided that it might be a good idea to bring some "real" student militants to London for a major television show, glorifying the

achievements of the New Left. The gathering was widely publicized. Not only did the visiting New Leftists make the front
pages, but they were also written up in the book sections, the
feature sections—and even the women's page. Penguin Books
rushed several left-wing manifestos into print. The posters that
had inflamed the French students in May were published in a
cheap paperback. Shaggy German radicals and hip American
demonstrators were transformed into folk heroes.

Cohn-Bendit, who was by this time putting on a great deal of
weight, represented France; and Tarik Ali, who was no longer
even a student, was the spokesman for Britain's student population. They mouthed their insipid dogmatisms, called upon Britain's students to revolt, and departed, leaving their stench behind them. It was now fashionable at most British universities
to mouth the cliches of the New Left, and Oxford students
rapidly acquiesced to the new spirit of the times. Hair became
longer, beards became more popular, clothing became slop-
pier. Within a week of the BBC broadcast the walls of many of
Oxford's oldest colleges were covered with the sort of slogans
one had observed at the University of Paris.

The growing group of student rebels founded an organization
called the Marcuse Society. They were itching for a confrontation. The following term they finally hit upon what they most
disliked about Oxford. It turned out to be All Souls College, an
elite institution, rather like Princeton's Institute for Advanced
Studies, where some of the best minds in Britain held fellowships. All Souls was purely a society of fellows; it had no undergraduates, and no plans for including them. This outraged the
Marcuse Society, which by this time had decided that All Souls
should be turned into a school for working-class youth. The All
Souls fellows, the society argued, were fat old men who sat
around drinking vintage port all day and did no work. The
leftists singled out All Souls' urbane warden, John Sparrow, for
particularly nasty treatment, ascribing to him every imagina-
ble vice.

155

But All Souls' academic excellence was such that it managed to endure all the picketing and name calling with the grace one has always associated with British institutions of higher learning. One particularly famous scholar, a towering man, even went so far as to confront the Marcuseans on his way to All Souls' common room, and to ask them what they wanted. After listening to their charges, he turned to the group's leader and declared: "Why you vulgar little man. You know nothing about All Souls." He then wrenched the picket sign away from one of the young revolutionaries and carried it off with him to the common room as a kind of war trophy. I am told that the sign remained in the common room for some weeks, and was the object of much comment.

All Souls was only the start. In the months that followed students gathered to protest all manner of things, from a visiting South African cricket team (they tore up the cricket pitch) to the fact that there weren't enough underprivileged people attending Oxford. While the rebels never gained the kind of authority they wanted, never ever really achieving a genuinely violent uprising, they did succeed in transforming a good and quiet university into a place where minor uprisings could be expected at any moment. Oxford was transformed into something different from what it had been before 1968. "It becomes more like an American university all the time," one of my old mentors remarked to me recently. He added, sadly, "Sic transit gloria mundi."

VI

The situation was, of course, worse in other British universities—much worse. The London School of Economics, and the universites of Sussex, Hull, Essex, and Leicester were seriously afflicted with varying degrees of campus unrest. Some of the student rebels complained about inadequate facilities, bad food, shoddy rooms, and the like; but the real reason for the rebellion of course had nothing to do with any of these problems: rebellion was simply the thing to do, it was *in*. Organizations like the Radical Student Alliance and the Revolutionary Socialist Students' Federation exploited the fact that rebellion was in vogue with great expertise. There were massive anti-American demonstrations throughout Britain. MPs from both the Labour and the Conservative parties were often shouted down whenever they appeared at universities, and in some cases they were even roughed up by campus mobsters. An American diplomat was soaked with red paint by students at Sussex, where American students played a leading role in radicalizing the university population. It was all very sad.

The historian D. C. Watt noted that British educationists had, like their American cousins, one goal in common with the student radicals: utilitarianism. The educationists wanted graduates who were trained to serve the instrumental needs of the state; the radicals wanted to see graduates who could serve the instrumental needs of the revolution. The British universities, he noted, were being narrowed down to the sort of institutes of managerial training that technocrats like M. Servan-Schreiber admired. And, he added, all this damage was being done by "a generation of academics moulded by the 1940s into accepting the State as an all-providing milch-cow to be managed by the processes of modern politics; a generation which in its innocence was unable to see its own *desiderata* as separate from those of public interest, and looked forward, starry-eyed, to a world in which university claims for money would outrank those of hospitals, elementary and secondary schools, housing and defense, a world in which all their ideas would be implementable, a world of academic frustration, a world in which universities would govern themselves, pursue their own ends, build and expand, for ever and ever into a golden future."[11]

11. D. C. Watt, "Expansion at the L. S. E.," *Fight for Education: A Black Paper,* ed. C. B. Cox and A. E. Dyson (London: Critical Quarterly Society, 1969), p. 34.

All this Dr. Watt saw as folly and, in a very real sense, as a betrayal of the university's fundamental ethos and interest. Expanding upon Watt's thesis that British universities, like American universities, were letting unqualified students into their confines for instrumental purposes, Kingsley Amis noted,

> Demands for student participation conceal . . . a simple desire to have less studying to do, less of everything that relates in any way to studying. As a consequence of irresponsible expansionism, the universities today are full of students who do not understand what study is all about, and who are painfully bewildered by the whole business and purpose of university life; *more has meant worse.* Student unrest has several causes, but here and now the prime one seems to me to be the presence in our universities of an academically-unfit majority, or large minority.[12] [Italics added]

In a plea for a renaissance of standards, Watt declared that the universities have passed

> over an opportunity to raise their standards of selection of students in favor of an expansion of numbers such as to disrupt their own intellectual cohesion and render it impossible for them even to give the extra students the same standard of attention enjoyed by their existing students! Now that their intellectual overindulgence has led to all the internal disorders which normally accompany obesity, the universities face a long, enforced fast in a world of financial famine and student unrest on a regular and increasingly ulcerous scale quite unlike the occasional hiccoughs of the past.

Now that Britain, like America, has experienced the insanity of student unrest there is little for serious scholars like Dr. Watt to feel happy about. But they can at least take some solace in the fact that to date no British university has experienced the kind of violence that has become so common in America. That's not much, but it's something.

12. Kingsley Amis, "Pernicious Participation," *ibid.,* p. 10.

Conditions were much more serious in France, where students actually had some grievances against an archaic system of education that was itself the child of revolution, the French Revolution. But before the uprising at the Nanterre campus of the University of Paris in 1968, things had been relatively quiet in France. The student left was in decline. It was a pale shadow of what it had been in the stormy days when France was fighting in Vietnam and Algeria, when the UNEF (the French National Federation of Students) played a role not unlike that of the SDS in the United States, only with much greater success. In those days left-wing goon squads policed the Latin Quarter, and it was virtually impossible for moderate French students to express themselves politically.

There were several serious problems in French higher education, particularly in Paris. Because of the system of open enrollment to any student with a high school *baccalauréat,* there was terrible overcrowding in the entire university system. Things were so bad that the great majority of students in Paris couldn't even get into the Sorbonne's lecture halls. They either had to stand in the streets and listen to those lectures that were broadcast over loudspeakers, or had to rely on printed collections of lectures delivered by their professors during the previous year. French professors hardly ever change their lecture notes; it was therefore possible to get through university without ever attending a class, simply by reading old lecture notes. Of course, there was virtually no contact between students and professors.

The course of instruction was rigidly old-fashioned, conforming to precepts designed by the Ministry of Education in the nineteenth century. Unless you were lucky enough (or, rather, smart enough) to get into one of the so-called Grand Schools, such as the École Normale or the École Polytechnique, it was almost impossible to get a truly first-rate education.

159

Many leftist French students looked to America's less formal universities as models for what they hoped French universities might one day become. Despite the fact that French intellectuals were already beginning to hold American institutions up to the French establishment as examples of what the twentieth century ought to be all about, the French establishment resisted Americanization. Indeed, French education was the least Americanized educational system in Europe.

But the American challenge manifested itself in different ways in France. Despite the spirit of anti-Americanism that pervades the French intellectual establishment, the French, more than any other European people, consciously strove to emulate America. The results were often very amusing. In the late fifties, for example, the so-called *nouvelle vague* film directors decided to model themselves after such second-rate American film directors as Jerry Lewis and Samuel B. Fuller. The end results were invariably disastrous.

Another example of distorted French Americanization is the craze for American drugstores, a craze which began in the early sixties. An enterprising businessman decided that the true spirit of American life was to be found in the sort of drugstores that existed in America during the thirties and forties and the French sought to re-create them. What they created, in fact, were a series of rather vulgar, overly posh, very French hot dog stands, bearing not even the foggiest resemblance to anything American. The main point, for the French, of course, was that they thought all this nonsense was American, and so they greatly enjoyed it. So too with the student militants who looked to the American left for motivation. They got many ideas from America but, like the "drugstore" entrepreneurs, they distorted whatever they got.

The events of 1968 began at Nanterre, which was a model new university, suffering from many of the same problems that rack other new universities throughout the world. To begin with, it was far from the center of Paris. There were no movie

160

houses, no theaters, and, what was worse, no good cafes in which the students could plot. Its buildings were cold and modern, but no worse than the cold and modern buildings of many new American universities. The faculty was perhaps the most radical of any in France, but the rules and regulations were perhaps the most medieval. Trouble began when a student was tossed out for visiting a girl's room. University rules declared that girls could visit boys' rooms, but not the other way around. "That way," the rector noted, "the university cannot be held responsible for anything the boys and girls do together."

Cohn-Bendit, who was to become the leader of the student left, was not the sort of student one would expect to find leading a French revolution. To begin with, he was not even French— he was, of all things, a German, although he had spent most of his life in France. He was rather plump and ordinary-looking, save for his bright red hair, which was to give added meaning to his nickname, Danny the Red. He was not an outstanding student, nor was he much of a public speaker. Indeed, had it not been for a confrontation he was to have with a member of de Gaulle's cabinet he might never have been noticed.

On a warm day in March 1968, the minister of sport was visiting Nanterre to open a new swimming pool. At the pool he was surrounded by a group of students, who engaged him in argument. "What do you want us to do for you?" he asked. At this point Cohn-Bendit stepped forward and declared, "We want you to do something for our sex lives." The minister was taken aback. "When I was your age," he smiled, "I would take a cold swim." He pointed to the pool. It was the wrong answer. The following day Cohn-Bendit was written up in most of the French newspapers. The minister's witty aside was held up as yet another example of official ignorance of student problems.

Later in March, students at Nanterre started demonstrating. Cohn-Bendit had become their leader and rallying point. After taking over some dormitories, the authorities called the feared CRS, the elite French riot police, who responded to the situation with that unique brand of brutality and stupidity for which they are universally known. Aside from clubbing the student demonstrators, they attacked innocent spectators, and even faculty members, and succeeded only in making matters worse. Now there was a genuine excuse for a revolution. The spark of Nanterre quickly spread to the Latin Quarter, and within a few weeks a minor rebellion at a minor university had become a problem of grave national concern. Even high school students took to the streets in solidarity with their brothers in the universities. During this entire period General de Gaulle behaved as if nothing serious were happening. He even went off to Romania to meet with that country's Communist leaders. During his absence the University of Paris was seized by the radicals. Professors were brutally beaten. The police fought hard against armed students to take back the university, but without success. The French Stock Exchange was invaded, and the famed Théâtre de l'Odeon was occupied.

This was the most serious rebellion France had faced since the days of Algeria, when Secret Army terrorists roamed the streets of every major French city. Things went from bad to worse, and there was every reason to believe that the students might in fact get their revolution and bring down President de Gaulle, whom they profoundly disliked. But the Communist Party refused to play their game, thus depriving the students of the kind of organization and working-class support they so dearly needed. The Communists had been doing rather well within the confines of the parliamentary system, and they had no desire to see things ruined by a student-led "ultraleftist" revolution. *L'Humanité,* the official Communist newspaper, blasted the students on all fronts, calling them Trotskyites and hooligans. The students felt betrayed. The Communists, Cohn-Bendit countered, had become "obsolete."

The Communist Party's refusal to give aid and support to the students was not the only problem standing between them and their revolution. Like radical students throughout the world,

162

the French students lacked a coherent ideology. They had no specific goals, no programs. They weren't even sure *why* they wanted a revolution. All they knew was that they wanted a revolution—a revolution for the sake of a revolution. When a *Le Monde* journalist asked Cohn-Bendit what his revolutionary goals were, he was shocked to learn that the young revolutionary was not interested in such questions. "First we must have a revolution. Then we can start talking about goals."

During the entire uprising only Premier Pompidou seemed to keep his head. There was talk about President de Gaulle's being out of touch, even senile. Why, people asked, had he left the country in a time of great crisis? When it was quite clear that the very foundations of the French Republic were being shaken, de Gaulle decided to cut short his visit to Romania. "The students," he declared upon his return, "are messing their own pants." That was his only comment. But under pressure from Pompidou he agreed to address the French nation—over the radio, since the television broadcast facilities were not available because of the intervention of striking technicians.

Before addressing the nation de Gaulle made a secret flight to the headquarters of General Massu, the French NATO commander. The army's support was vital, and de Gaulle knew that many sectors of the military had never forgiven him for granting Algerian independence. A deal was struck. In return for army support, if needed, de Gaulle would free all the Secret Army leaders, and allow such right-wing critics of his regime as Jacques Soustelle to return to France and resume their political activities. With the support of the military behind him, de Gaulle could appeal to the French people from a position of strength. He recognized that they were weary of violence and disorder. He also knew that they feared a return to the kind of chaos that existed before his return to power.

His appeal was for "law and order." There would be a general election, and violence would no longer be tolerated. The people rallied behind de Gaulle, and staged counterdemonstrations against the students. When the general election came around, de Gaulle, and particularly Pompidou, who had masterminded the entire strategy, received a massive vote of confidence, which was also a clear rebuke to the students. It was to be a time for the healing of wounds, for order and calm. The students left their universities for their summer vacations. Cohn-Bendit was sent back to his native Germany, still huffing and puffing about revolutionary action. The revolution of May is not yet over, he warned. "Ce n'est qu'un début, continuons le combat!" Nevertheless, things seemed to be returning to normal and, for the time being, the French breathed a collective sigh of relief.

Since 1968 there have been numerous reforms throughout the French educational system. Many of the problems that existed at the time of the Paris uprising no longer exist. No doubt the disciples of Professor Marcuse will write the reforms off as yet another example of "repressive tolerance." Cohn-Bendit may well have been correct when he declared the events of 1968 to be only the beginning of a new and more general revolution. Certainly the Paris uprising revealed real and dangerous problems that may well succeed in afflicting France in the future. Today a very large slice of the French student population, particularly at the elite Paris institutions, has been radicalized. True to the spirit of the absent Cohn-Bendit, the radicals are well to the left of the French Communist Party. In fact, it is worth noting that the major student demonstration of 1972 was an anti-Communist demonstration. The student right, such as it is, is in many ways every bit as extreme in its methods as the student left, and several rightist organizations have been outlawed for bombing and street fighting.

At the height of the 1968 violence, one of the most quoted student slogans declared, "Plus je fais l'amour, plus j'ai envie de faire la Révolution; plus je fais la révolution, plus j'ai envie de faire l'amour." It may not sound like Lenin or Stalin, but many observers of the contemporary French scene view such jolly slogans with far greater trepidation than anything else contained in the often sterile catechisms of the Old Left. France has not seen the last of her revolting students.

VIII

Nowhere in Western Europe have things been as bad as they are in Germany today. West German students are the most radical in contemporary Europe. They are also the most Americanized. Indeed, American influence has been the prime factor in the postwar history of West Germany. It has not simply been a classroom experience. From the Armed Forces Radio and Television broadcasting network that reaches into the homes of most West Germans, to the presence of American soldiers, big business, and, most important, American ideology, the Germans have felt the impact of the American image more thoroughly than any other European people.

In 1945 Germany was divided in two, the Eastern part going to Stalin's victorious legions, the Western part to the Allies; the Eastern part to Stalinist totalitarianism, the Western part to parliamentary democracy. This division of Germany into two separate political entities is the central element in the life of postwar Germany. Dissent was not tolerated in the so-called German Democratic Republic in the East, and such dissenters as did exist either escaped into West Germany or were brutally and firmly silenced by the Soviets and their puppets. In the German Federal Republic of the West, dissent was not only allowed, but actually encouraged. The West Germans were to be democratized, and West Germany was to be a paradigm of modern democracy, where the advantages of the capitalist system over communism were to be clearly observed and noted by all who were interested. There was to be no return to Nazi militarism. If the older generation was permanently tainted with the lingering scars of the Hitlerian madness, the younger

165

generation, it was hoped, would lead Germany into a new and constructive era of freedom and justice for all. This was to be achieved through education. The older generation could only be rehabilitated, but the youth were to be *educated*—or to put it more bluntly, *Americanized.*

Originally it was feared that the division of Germany would itself bring about a revival of German nationalism, and other latent extremist elements; and, indeed, there were Germans who were only too willing to use Germany's divided status as an excuse for their own political extremism. But most thoughtful Germans turned away from political extremism towards the concept of a strong and united Europe. Good Germans, Dr. Konrad Adenauer argued, must first be good Europeans. The European Economic Community welcomed German membership, as did the North Atlantic Treaty Organization. The Germans were bound and determined to become respectable again. The German left, embodied in the Social Democrat Party, was pro-European, firmly anti-Communist, and, as one writer put it, "soft on capitalism."

In the fifties the German economy boomed. There was a renaissance of German culture. It was a time of healing for Germany, and many Germans looked forward to the future with great hope. But in the sixties West Germany began to experience the kind of serious problems that were hurting other European nations. The decade began with the erection of the Berlin Wall, a monument that served to symbolize the permanence of Germany's division. The city of Berlin, which had long been a helpless pawn in the Cold War, came to personify the struggle between the United States and the Soviets. The Economic Miracle of the fifties began to slow down, although by no means too seriously.

Because of the numerous Berlin crises, the Social Democrats found their first popular postwar leader in that city's anti-Communist mayor, Willy Brandt. The once unquestioned leadership of the Christian Democrat Party began to falter, partly

166

because of social conditions, mainly because of the power vacuum left by Dr. Adenauer's retirement. With the political situation becoming chaotic, a Grand Coalition of the Christian Democrats and the Socialists was formed in 1966. If any one development can be said to have helped trigger student rebellion in Germany, it was the Grand Coalition. Now the West German parliament was to be dominated by two parties, united in purpose. There were no longer any outlets for political eccentrics, especially on the left.

The Social Democrat Party, which had always tolerated a small but vocal group of left-wing extremists, was now in league with the conservative Christian Democrat Party. For the political extremists, this proved that the two major parties were really the same, that there was no room for them within the parliamentary process. The left thought that the Socialists had sold out to the conservatives; the extreme right thought that the Christian Democrats had sold out to the Marxists. Germany, the extremists cried out, had become a conformist society that would not tolerate their particular brand of political nonconformism.

Since the Christian Democrats were the senior partners in the Grand Coalition, the right-wing reaction was not as strong as the left-wing reaction. Germany was still being ruled by a fundamentally conservative government. For a short period of time the extreme National Democratic Party of Adolf "Bubbi" von Thadden challenged the Grand Coalition from the right, but the NDP quickly broke apart under tremendous pressures from the press, and because of the stupidity of its leader. Things were different on the left, The Sozialistischer-Deutsche-Studentbund, or the SDS (not to be confused with the American SDS), emerged as an effective and highly disciplined antiparliamentary movement. Parliament, the SDS argued, was nothing but a charade, and the politicians of both major parties were social perverts.

German students tend to be much older than American students. They move from university to university, which is a German tradition, and remain in university until they feel they are ready to take their examinations. This may take as long as ten years, and, in many cases, even longer. So in Germany there is a genuine student class. Of the 280,000 university students in West Germany, barely five percent come from working-class backgrounds. Among the student rebels, almost everyone is middle or upper-middle class.

The position of the SDS has never been very clear. Ideologically, it discovered Herbert Marcuse before he was ever widely known in the United States, but that tells little about its actual positions on specific issues. The Social Democrat Party, argued the SDS, had embraced capitalism and anticommunism, and the SDS was both anticapitalist and pro-Communist. Beyond that its main hate was Mr. Axel Springer, the powerful and very conservative West German newspaper publisher, whose papers have persistently exposed the SDS to ridicule and attack. Indeed, actual student violence began in West Germany in 1967 with a raid on Mr. Springer's Berlin office. Violence continued throughout that year. Vice President Hubert Humphrey, on a visit to Berlin, was pelted with sacks of flour, and after he left that city, the Shah of Iran received the same treatment.

But all this was literally fun and games. The militant student left lacked both a platform and a leader. It never found its platform, but it did find a leader in Rudi Dutschke, a fanatical former East German, who had come to the Free University of Berlin, the main center of West German student activism, to study, of all things, theology. Dutschke was a brilliant rabble-rouser, and his calls for student violence spread throughout Germany's student population. Under his leadership, university buildings throughout Germany were seized, along with buildings belonging to the Springer newspapers. His followers surged through the streets of Berlin chanting "Ho-Che-Du, Ho-Che-Du," for Ho Chi Minh, Che Guevara, and Dutschke himself. Many Germans feel that Dutschke was on the verge of becoming one of the most influential figures in West German politics. But in April of 1968, Dutschke, the advocate of student violence, was shot in the head by a right-wing student, and hasn't been politically active since.

Meanwhile, German left-wing students have pioneered in new techniques of violence. While the SDS continues to shout down professors and beat up political moderates, rendering many German universities inoperable, the more extreme Red Army Faction bombs and kills. Led by Andreas Baader and Ulrike Meinhof, the Red Army has shot American soldiers outside the United States Army European Command Headquarters, and blown up the officers' casino at the U.S. Fifth Army Corps in Frankfurt, killing an American colonel and wounding others. Other targets for Red Army bombings have included police stations, the Hamburg plant of Axel Springer, and the law courts. The Red Army has modeled itself after the American Weathermen.

The future looks very dark for German higher education today. Although the student radicals remain a minority at most universities, they are strong enough to close their institutions down at will. If they don't like what a professor is teaching, the professor may well be beaten. They are often aided by allies on the faculty, and by the inability of the authorities to cope with the situation. Worst of all is the Free University of Berlin, America's gift to Germany. It has long since ceased to be a university, and has become a training ground for student leftists. Perhaps the saddest comment one can make about West Germany's universities is that they have become vastly inferior to East Germany's universities. The West Germans can thank their student rebels for this.

IX

Student unrest has become a fact of life throughout the free world. In Japan, Holland, Italy, Spain, Portugal, Brazil, and Argentina, a very substantial number of students have chosen the path of revolution, and are working with great skill to destroy their universities and, consequently, to bring about revolutions in their respective countries. The similarities between the various student rebels and their movements are perhaps the most startling aspects of this phenomenon. Student rebellion is nothing new, especially in Europe and Latin America; but the older generation of student rebels varied from country to country, and even from university to university. Despite the rhetoric of the "Internationale," student rebels in the past were divided by language, culture, and ideology. Today language is no longer a problem thanks to the rapidity of translation and the near universal understanding of English; cultural differences, especially among students, have been wiped out thanks to the impact of the modern mass media; and the ideology of the New Left is so vague that it can be applied to almost any situation.

The position of America in the modern world is akin to that of Paris in eighteenth-century France. Just as Parisian fads, books, ideas, and styles were emulated throughout France, even in the most provincial backwaters, so today are American ideas, fads, and styles imitated throughout the rest of the world, only with even greater impact. The student left, despite the fact that it varies slightly from country to country in its style and influence, has been as strongly influenced by America as everything else in the world. Indeed, when the BBC brought left-wing students from several European and American countries together in 1968, it was hard to tell one from another. They all agreed with one another on every fundamental issue, they even dressed the same and used the same slang. Their political and intellectual heroes (aside from Ho and Che) were mainly

Americans. Malcolm X, H. Rap Brown, Herbert Marcuse, Noam Chomsky, C. Wright Mills, and Angela Davis are as influential in Europe as they are in America.

The student movement is not without its weaknesses. Perhaps the movement's greatest weakness is its transient nature. Students are only in a university situation for a short period of time. When old student militants leave for the real world, fresh converts must be found to fill the gaps left by departing comrades. This despite the fact that many militants tend to linger around their old universities for several years after graduating or being flunked out. The movement's other main weakness is its lack of general appeal outside the academic world. It simply has no support from the general public. The various Communist parties and trade union movements, from which the student militants quite naturally would expect to find support, have consistently refused to work with the students, and have even worked against them. All this may be attributed, at least in part, to the fact that the students really don't seem to stand for very much beyond some vague concept of revolution for its own sake. Real revolutionaries tend to look upon them as a bunch of silly kids freaked out on a kind of ideological panty raid.

What the future of the student left will be remains to be seen. It may not get its revolution, at least in the affluent societies of the West, but it almost certainly will cause a lot of damage along the way. As for the militants themselves, their future will be on the left, even if they moderate slightly as they mature. Some, no doubt, will be reformed by the pressures of the real world outside the universities. Others will join the establishment left, becoming good social democrats and even good Communists. The minority will remain hard-core fanatics. Nevertheless, whatever their individual future may be, they will have succeeded in seriously damaging the universities of the world.

Jean-Francois Revel is correct when he says that the real

revolution of our time is an American revolution. America has given birth to a new and often dangerous left-wing movement that has spread from our campuses to those of nearly every major university in the free world. This New Left phenomenon has posed a serious challenge to culture and learning throughout the world, and has led educators to question the ability of their universities to survive at all. Let us hope that America will lead the way in taming this menace to the survival of higher learning. That would be a worthy legacy to future generations, for if the New Left is not stopped very soon, it may be too late for higher learning. It may already be too late.

8

Conclusion

SINCE THE EARLIEST DAYS OF THE REPUBLIC, AMERICANS have turned
to their schools and universities for solutions to the many complex problems that have historically distressed our society.
Education has always been held in high esteem by most Americans, but rarely, if ever, have we valued it as a thing unto itself.
Rather, the ancillary products of education, such as its ability
to influence society as a whole, were the things we *really*
prized. We saw our schools and universities not so much instruments of education, as the building blocks of America. Quantity
became more important than quality, and, as a result, American education—while appearing, on the surface, to be strong
and healthy—failed to develop the respect for academic standards so apparent in the schools and universities of nations
beyond our shores. Under these circumstances it became increasingly difficult for American institutions of learning to
fulfill the primary function of education, the *bringing up,*
through systematic instruction in certain fundamental moral
and intellectual *disciplines,* of the youth; and American education relentlessly devalued its academic standards, chucking all
intellectual pretense, and transforming our schools and universities into instruments of sociological reformation.

We have spent vast sums of time and money on education,
and have constructed the most enormous educational complex
in human history. Nevertheless—despite our great proliferation of educational institutions—our schools and colleges re-

main, as they have always been, marginal to the rest of our society. Because of their marginal position, our educational institutions have never managed to live up to our sociological expectations. In fact, they have always been better at *creating* social problems than *solving* them. Still, as Professor Christopher Jencks and his colleagues at Harvard's Center for Educational Policy Research have recently reminded us, no amount of evidence to the contrary can dissuade most Americans from the belief that educational institutions exist primarily to solve social problems.[1]

Our educational system, as that perceptive writer Albert Jay Nock has noted, was founded, in all good faith, on the assumption that universal elementary and secondary education would create a society that was both equal and intelligent.[2] It has failed to make us either more equal or more intelligent. "The general level of intelligence in our citizenry," wrote Nock, "stands exactly where it stood when the system was established. The promoters of our system . . . did not know . . . that the average age at which the development of intelligence is arrested lies somewhere between twelve and thirteen years. It is with intelligence as with eyesight. No oculist can give one any more eyesight than one has; he can only regulate what one has. . . . Education can only regulate what intelligence one has, . . . it cannot give one any more. . . . As for raising the general level of intelligence, the sluicing-out of any amount of education on our citizenry would simply be pouring water on a duck's back."[3] For all its good intentions, our educational system has failed even in its egalitarian desires. Our schools, Christopher Jencks has sadly concluded, have few long-term effects on the

1. Christopher Jencks, *Inequality: A Reassessment of the Effect of Family and Schooling in America* (New York: Basic Books, 1972). Jencks and his colleagues at Harvard have reexamined most of the egalitarian dogmas held by educationist reformers, and found them to be wanting.
2. A.J. Nock, *The Memoirs of a Superfluous Man* (Chicago: Henry Regnery, 1964), p. 261.
3. *Ibid.*, p. 261.

equality, intelligence, or worldly success of those who attend them.

One searches in vain through the writings of nineteenth-century American educators for a Cardinal Newman or a Matthew Arnold. From Thomas Jefferson and Horace Mann to the young John Dewey, all one encounters are egalitarian tinkerers who view education only in instrumentalist or sociological terms. Often their motives vary: Jefferson's approach to universal education was founded upon his physiocratic prejudices; Mann, on the other hand, based his educational philosophy on the dubuious "science" of phrenology, which he called "the only practical basis for education."[4] Both viewed the schools as *sociological unifiers* first, and *educational* institutions second. Jefferson's eighteenth-century mind focused on the need for educating the yeomanry of his region; Mann's vision was more comprehensive, embracing the whole of American society. Where Jefferson yearned to bring the small landowners of Virginia into the mainstream of America, Mann hoped to create a common American culture, which would make all Americans alike, and assimilate the disparate immigrant children, then just beginning to come to our shores, into his version of the American "melting pot." Assimilation and sociological homogenization were to become more important than education.

Assimilationism did not come to dominate American educational thought overnight. In the early years of the nineteenth century, such opponents of assimilationism as the eloquent Catholic polemicist Orestes Brownson argued passionately in favor of localism and educational voluntarism, stressing the importance of community and local control over education.[5]

4. Quoted in Jonathan Messerli's *Horace Mann: A Biography* (New York: Alfred A. Knopf, 1972), p. 351. Mann had read George Combe's phrenological treatise, *The Constitution of Man Considered in Relation to External Objects* (Boston, 1841), and became convinced that the Combean theory of phrenology vindicated the ways of God to man. "We see," wrote Mann, "that there will be a new earth . . . if not a new heaven, when [phrenology] prevails."
5. Michael B. Katz, *Class, Bureaucracy, and School: The Illusion of Educational Change in America* (New York: Frederick A. Praeger, 1971), pp. 3–56.

Mann and his followers, Brownson argued, ignored the unique variety of American cultural life, and wished to destroy that variety by imposing a uniform culture on a diverse clientele. The only way that the advocates of the public common schools could get the discordant poor to send their children to those schools, Bishop John Hughs noted, was to pass laws depriving parents of public relief unless their children were immediately enrolled. "Yet, after all this," Hughs bitterly declared, "they pretend to have the confidence of the poor." In the reforms of the assimilationists, Brownson saw the death of freedom of instruction, adding, "adieu to republicanism, to social progress." "We may as well have a religion established by law," Brownson wrote, "as a system of education, and the government educate and appoint the pastors of our churches, as well as the instructors of our children."

Mann countered, by declaring, "If one man claimed to have his peculiar doctrines taught, why not another? Why not all?—until you would have a Babel of creeds in the same school, which a heathen would be ashamed of." To Mann, as Michael Katz has noted, educational reform was not simply a job, it was a *cause*. Indeed, at the heart of educational reform in America, there has been, historically, a kind of evangelistic zeal, predicated on certain environmental and social presumptions about the nature and destiny of man. The presumptions were all optimistic, permeated with the idea of progress. Assimilation had to win out in the end, Mann noted, in a letter to Barnard, because "it is a part of my religion." He even went so far as to liken himself and his task to Peter the Hermit, championing the Crusades. In truth, Mann was no Peter the Hermit; rather, he combined in his person the two main types of provincialism —bitterness and smugness—which Matthew Arnold dubbed Hebraism.

Nevertheless, Mann and the assimilationist advocates of the the common culture were to prevail in the long run. Mann's Hebraizing crusade was to succeed precisely because, as Arnold had noted in his preface to *Culture and Anarchy,* the

176

people of the United States were products of the Hebraizing middle class. "From Maine to Florida," Arnold wrote, "America Hebraises." Where Arnold thought education ought to produce "sweetness and light," the American Hebraizers were concerned only with assimilation and the production of students trained in utilitarian skills. The assimilating side of Mann's gospel appealed to our native optimism, which was Protestant in origin (that is, the Arminian brand, which the Great Awakening had failed to expunge from the American character); the utilitarianism was simply a manifestation of a native pragmatism, which had no use for anything lacking in instrumental value.

After a period of struggle with the forces of educational conservatism, the assimilationist utilitarianism of Mann and his disciples triumphed. To the present day, whether under the banner of forced integration or busing, or some other assimilationist nostrum, it continues to hold sway over the American educational scene. While the emphasis on assimilation and utilitarianism has as little to do with true education today as it did in Mann's time, the advocates of this position can say, with Mann, that true education is beside the point: the school's chief purpose is to solve social problems. Indeed, the arguments and conclusions of Professor Coleman's *Equality of Educational Opportunity* and the Civil Rights Commission's study *Racial Isolation in the Public Schools,* about environmental and cultural deprivation, are similar in tone, if not language, to the writings of the nineteenth-century assimilationists.

On the purely pedagogical level, the twentieth century introduced several educational innovations that were every bit as revolutionary—and *detrimental*—as anything advocated by Mann. Under the banner of progressive education—itself a convenient label for almost all early twentieth-century educational reforms—serious humanistic scholars were banished from the schools. There place was taken by the "professional educationists"—a new breed of schoolmen, trained in teachers colleges as opposed to liberal arts colleges, specializing in educational administration and pedagogy for pedagogy's sake. In a very short period of time, these educationists came to control most of our schools, and all of our teacher-training institutions.[6]

The progressives emphasized the need for relating the child's experiences to the curriculum. Pupils were encouraged to participate more in the learning process, and course content and teaching methods were altered to achieve this end. But progressive education was not at all individualistic. Dewey, the most intelligent of the progressives, accentuated the predominance of the group over the individual. In this, progressive education shared one of the basic tenets of the progressive political movement, which also downgraded the role of the individual will in relation to that of the community as a whole. Most important, in terms of long-run influence, the progressives, like their nineteenth-century predecessors, and their most recent heirs, held that education was first and last a key to social mobility, that the school could help to solve society's problems.

The assimilationist tendencies of the nineteenth century, which eventually evolved into the progressive movement in the early years of the twentieth century, really came into their own during the 1960s. Under the guise of "problem-solving," the schools became the loci of a massive movement to redress a number of profound social problems that had plagued our society throughout its history. In practically every case, the most recent attempts to reform society through the schools have not only failed, but often backfired. One need only cite the crusade to end racial discrimination through scholastic integration and, later, busing. The sociological fall-out from the Coleman report, along with the recent studies of David Armour and others, provides ample evidence to demonstrate that racial discord

6. See James D. Koerner, *The Case for Basic Education* (Boston: Little, Brown & Co., Atlantic Monthly Press, 1959), pp. vii–ix.

in America is worse today than it was in the 1950s. Indeed, we need not even read the writings of the social scientists to see this point; all we have to do is look around, and observe how—despite the good intentions of the social reformers—race relations have deteriorated.

I have mentioned the movement to achieve racial integration through the schools, only because it provides us with a recent "ideal type" for the kind of social engineering that has dominated American education since the days of Horace Mann. Integration was held to be good, because it was another way of assimilating people into the common culture envisaged by reforming educationists. Since the nineteenth century, educationist reformers have held that inequality and sociological variety are at the root of our nation's social problems. The solution to those problems has been their main aim, and from Mann to Conant their solution has been the creation of an egalitarian common culture. To date, they have only succeeded in botching up American education. Christopher Jencks and his colleagues have concluded that education cannot solve our social problems, and that it is high time that the social reformers look elsewhere for the solutions to society's problems. The educators ought to leave social reform to the social reformers, and get back to the business of educating the youth.

II

The conflict that exists between ability and the idea of equality of opportunity is at the heart of the present crisis in American education.[7] When the Founding Fathers talked about

7. In his book *Inequality*, p. 3, Christopher Jencks writes: "Most Americans say they believe in equality. But when pressed to explain what they mean by this, their definitions are usually full of contradictions. Many will say, like the Founding Fathers, that 'all men are created equal.' Many will also say that all men are equal 'before God,' and that they are . . . equal in the eyes of the law. But most Americans also believe that some people are more competent than others, and that this will always be so, no matter how much we try to reform society."

equality, they meant something quite different from what we mean by the term today; they predicated their thought upon what was for them the "self-evident" concept of a *natural aristocracy* of virtue and talent. For them equality was a legal concept, which they understood to mean equality before the law. It was obvious to them that all men were not equal. "By the law of nature," John Adams wrote, "man differs . . . from man as much as from beast. . . . A physical inequality, an intellectual inequality, of the most serious kind, is established unchangeably by the Author of nature." When Thomas Jefferson wrote of the need to "diffuse" knowledge, he was not advocating an eighteenth-century version of open enrollment; he was simply calling for the improvement and expansion of the American educational enterprise. Jefferson, like Adams, founded his educational philosophy on the idea of a natural aristocracy.

Equality of opportunity has never meant that all men are physically or intellectually equal, despite the fact that many modern educationists have sought to interpret it in this way. It is obvious, as the French poet Paul Valéry once wrote, that if all men were equally enlightened, equally critical, and equally courageous, no society would be possible.[8] It is now clear, as Paul Seabury has recently noted, that equality of results, as opposed to equality of opportunity, is the new goal of the egalitarians.[9] The CCNY of pre-open-enrollment days operated under the principle of equality of opportunity, and the results were impressive; CCNY today, under open enrollment, operates under the principle of equality of results, and the consequences of this ignoble experiment are apparent to even the most casual observer. No one can deny that barriers to equality of opportunity based on race and religion have historically existed in our society, but, as Professor Seabury has wisely reminded us, those who stress equality of results over equality of opportunity

8. Cited by Paul Seabury in his lecture, "The Idea of Merit," *Commentary*, December 1972, p. 44.
9. *Ibid.*, pp. 43–45.

and merit are simply attempting to lead us into a new era of discrimination based on race and religion.

Under the banner of "affirmative action" a new kind of discrimination in favor of previously discriminated-against groups (such as blacks) has come into being. The new egalitarians who advocate equality of results over equality of opportunity now demand that quotas should be set so that various racial, sexual, and ethnic groupings can be represented proportionally in our schools and universities, regardless of ability. The advocates of this new egalitarianism seem not to recognize that they are setting up a system of reverse discrimination based on the same racial, sexual, and cultural categories as the old discrimination. Furthermore, they seem not to appreciate the extent to which they are hurting society as a whole. The lowering of standards to admit certain racial and ethnic groups to universities has not necessarily been beneficial to those groups. On the contrary, this destandardization, as we have earlier noted, has turned the academically unqualified members of those groups away from more useful pursuits by dangling before them a college degree as the key to their future success. The doctrine of equality of results, as the faculty at CCNY has sadly discovered, does not necessarily produce equality of results. Nor does it allow for the pursuit of excellence, which is so essential for the survival of society.

Since a modern society must produce skilled people in such technical fields as medicine, dentistry, engineering, etc., most of the destandardization presently afflicting our universities has taken place outside the technical subjects, in the so-called humanities' departments. Yet, in a society that has sought to assimilate all groups into a common culture through the schools, consequently lowering standards in the process, is it not fair to ask whether that society has a right to set high standards in certain subjects and no standards in other subjects? In theory, as Anthony Burgess has remarked, democratic societies ought to have the right to set academic standards democratically.[10] Yet no society, regardless of how democratic it is, would accept treatment from, say, medical doctors who had "done their own thing" in medical school. It is only in the humanities, Burgess laments, that "we can get away with a course in classics that asks no Latin or Greek . . . or [with] an in-depth survey of the prosody of Allen Ginsberg. The division between a scientific discipline and a humanistic laxness is already manifesting itself in undergraduate life styles. The banner-waving students who hold protest meetings are merely indulged. They will never rule America. . . . " If standards hold in the technical subjects—something that cannot absolutely be guaranteed in a society as destandardized as ours—America, Burgess asserts, may come under the control of "the hard-eyed technicians who have no time for protest."

Burgess, being a humanist, would have us return to an educational system that at least vaguely resembles the kind of rigor he knew as an undergraduate in Britain, a system in which he was expected to have "special distinctions in subjects like Latin, French and modern history," as well as in musical composition, hexameter writing, Italian, and Anglo-Saxon. He plainly resents the fact that at CCNY, where he was a visiting professor in 1972, functional illiterates were tossed into his English classes. The end result, he emphasizes, will not be a happy one for American society. "Inflation is at work everywhere," he concludes,

> and it is to be noted that the Ph.D. degree has become the minimal qualification for the full-fledged university teacher. Perhaps doctoral qualifications will have to be eased, following the democratic process. We are perhaps already in danger of seeing our existing universities turn into glorified high schools and superuniversities, specializing in real further education, emerging for the benefit of an elite. In the technical field this is happening already. And, when inflation overtakes the new superuniversities,

10. Anthony Burgess, "My Dear Students," *New York Times Magazine,* November 19, 1972, p. 30.

supersuperuniversities will have to be built. This can go on forever. Ultimately, the gods of learning are not mocked. The term "university" may be rich in noble connotations, but it means only what we want it to mean.[11]

This is certainly one of the possible end products of the movement for equality of results.

What is to be done about this? Paul Seabury has noted that in his home city, Berkeley, California, affirmative-action programs presently call for the abandonment of examinations, I.Q. tests, and other standards of intellectual measurement and certification.[12] "One proposal goes so far," he writes, "as to advocate that previous felony convictions not be considered in the employment of civil servants. Why, one wonders, do we not simply have recourse to a lottery?" Berkeley, of course, is a hideous caricature of the evils we have been dealing with; yet it reflects the grotesque reality of our educational and cultural crisis. For Berkeley, like most of the United States, longs for the common, integrated culture that Horace Mann dreamed about in the nineteenth century. Perhaps the best way out of our present situation is to take everything that is now being done in Professor Seabury's home city, and do just the opposite. Alas, what was once truistic now needs to be shouted from the housetops: within the circle of education, we *need* examinations, we *need* I.Q. tests, and, most of all, we *desperately need* a revival of old-fashioned academic standards.

The importance of the college education must be drastically deemphasized. We must have *fewer* but better universities, with *smaller* but better student bodies. At about the age of puberty, students with the potential to do well in universities should be separated from their less academically gifted fellows and sent to elitist high schools. Of course the decision of who should and who should not go to university cannot be made

11. *Ibid.,* p. 32.
12. Seabury, *op. cit.,* p. 45.

183

arbitrarily, and there should be leeway for so-called late-bloomers and idiot-savants. The decision to send students on to university must be made on the basis of merit, and merit alone. No extraneous element, such as race or sex, should be allowed to influence this decision. As for the nonacademic students, they should begin their career training at about the same time the academic students begin their precollege preparation. In some cases, paramedicine for example, this career education might take as many years as the achievement of a B.A. degree. But in many cases, the students should complete their career training at the time they would normally leave high school. Here too the standards must be rigorous, since considerable ability and intelligence will be needed for many of the career-training programs.

III

Professional educationists, Michael Katz has written, can still contribute a great deal to our society, "but the days when they should offer blueprints have ended." "Let us be thankful," he concludes, "for [the system they created] has brought us to where we are: Too many children do not learn well and are unhappy in school; teachers suffer and lack autonomy; parents are dissatisfied; and economists warn of impending massive unemployment. Not even a college degree assures one a job anymore. Aside from the people who live off the educational system . . . it has served no one very well. We are all its victims, and no one has done very much constructive about that for the last century."[13]

Whether American education will change for the better remains to be seen. More and more, individual educators, who once championed the reformist goals of the educational estab-

13. Katz, *op. cit.,* p. 152.

lishment, have come to see the futility of those goals, and the programs they engendered, but the establishment has a hundred defenders for each of its critics. Indeed, those who venture to criticize the educational establishment are, more often than not, exposed to all sorts of attacks. It is simply not in the interest of the establishment to tolerate criticism of its approach to education; it has a vested interest in preserving the status quo. Because of the educationists who make up our educational establishment, American education has become a cracked bell, devoid of harmony, and very likely beyond repair. If our educational system is to become great again it must reject its humanitarianism, and once again embrace those humane studies that are the essence of a true education. If this is done, there is hope for American education; but there is little reason to believe that it will be done.

Index

187

Handlin, Oscar, 101
Harvard, John, 28, 35
Harvard Crimson, 61
Harvard School of Business Administration, 37
Harvard University, 28, 30, 31, 32, 40, 51, 61, 91, 100, 103, 105, 108
Haskings, Charles Homer, 31, 40n
Hayek, F. A. von, 86, 121
Health, Education and Welfare, Department of, 96
Henry, William A., III, 103n
Higher Education Act, 103, 104, 117, 127–128, 132
Higher Education Facilities Act, 127
Hiss, Alger, 42
Hitchcock, James, 47n
Ho Chi Minh, 46, 168, 170
Hodgart, Matthew, 20n
Hoffman, Abbie, 41, 41n, 46
Hook, Sidney, 18, 42, 56
Howard University, 65, 67–88
Hughs, John, 176
Hull, University of, 156
Humphrey, Hubert, 168

Illinois, University of, 126
Indiana University, 64, 67–88
Innovations, 26, 101, 177
Instrumentalism, 33–35, 37, 146
Integration, racial, 179
  student opinion concerning, 75–76
Intercollegiate Studies Institute (ISI), 40
Israel, student opinion concerning, 76–77

Jay, John, 51n
Jefferson, Thomas, 28, 29, 32, 33, 34, 52, 175, 180
Jencks, Christopher, 174, 179
Jesus Christ, 143–144
Johnson, Lyndon, 62
Justman, Joseph, 129

Katz, Michael B., 175n, 176, 184
Keniston, Kenneth, 48
Kennedy, John F., 66
Keppel, Francis, 116, 118, 122, 130
Kerr, Clark, 60, 124–125, 127, 136, 151
Keynes, Lord, 66
Kilson, Martin, 100
Kings' College. *See* Columbia University

Kirk, Russell, 34
Koerner, James D., 126, 178n
Kopperman, Ralph, 100n
Kristol, Irving, 57
Krutch, Joseph Wood, quoted, 93

Land-grant colleges and universities, 126
Leary, Timothy, 145
Left, student, 40–46, 49, 56–57, 60, 73, 92, 148, 151, 153, 159
Leicester, University of, 156
Levi-Strauss, Claude, quoted, 27
Liberalism, 42, 62, 66, 90, 91, 134n
Life, 79
Lindsay, John V., 97
Lipset, Seymour Martin, 51n, 55–56, 57, 58n, 91
London School of Economics, 40n, 42, 153, 156
Luce, Henry, 140
Lunn, Sir Arnold, 76

Machlup, Fritz, 111
Malcolm X, 30, 43, 171
Manhattanville College, 101
Mann, Horace, 34, 35, 118, 175–177, 179, 183
Mao, 30, 45
Marcuse, Herbert, 30, 46, 58, 59, 145, 147–149, 152, 164, 168, 171
Marcuse Society, 155
Marland, Sidney P., 124, 130
Marquette University, 64, 67–88
Marx, Karl, 30, 37, 55, 58, 143–144
Marxism, 42
Massachusetts Institute of Technology (MIT), 126
Massachusetts School Act (1647), 27–28
Mather, Cotton, 30
Maude, Angus, 14
McCarthy, Eugene, 71
McCarthy, Joe, 42
McCarthy, Mary, 144
Meinhof, Ulrike, 169
Messerli, Jonathan, 175n
Middle East, student opinion concerning the, 76–77
Mill, John Stuart, 33, 121
Mills, C. Wright, 152, 171
Minnesota, University of, 126
More, Paul Elmer, 34
Morison, Samuel Eliot, 28n, 32n, 51

189

190